Designed

by

S.H Bando Press

Questions And Customer Service:
email us at bando13press@gmail.com

S.H
BANDO PRESS

This Journal Belongs To

....

The hunger and fullness scale

If you're familiar with (Mindful Eating), then you know about
the hunger and fullness scale, a toolto help you get in touch with your
hunger and fullness cues.

Here's how to use the HUNGER AND FULLNESS SCALE

   When you are getting ready to eat a meal or snack, ask yourself
"Where am I on the hunger and fullness scale?" Ideally, you'll be between a
and a 6.(the hunger scale, Choose to scale one meal every day)

   Halfway through your meal, pause for 10 seconds, and check in with your
body. Ask again "Where am I on the scale now?"

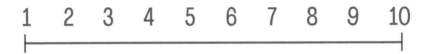

1 - Painfully hungry (nausea, upset stomach, etc) or sometimes so hungry
that you don't feel hungry anymore

2 - hangry (moody, cranky, highly irritated) with an empty pit in your
stomach that doesn't go away and is very distracting

3 - hungry(stomach rumbles, trouble focusing)thought of food more
frequently, feeling like you need energy

4 - I could eat, food thoughts come and go, stomach feels slightly empty

5 - neutral, not hungry or full

6 - stomach feels a little full but not totally satisfied, thoughts of food
less frequent

7 - stomach a little full but a comfortable satisfied, ready to take on your
next task

8 - full and don't want anything else to eat

9 - change into your yoga pants uncomfortable full or unbutton the top
button kind of full, may feel sleepy

10 - extremely uncomfortably full to the point of nausea feeling sick

How to use:Example

Date: 9/7/2021   Sleep Time: 7 hours   😄 ☺ 😐 ☹ 😫

☕ Breakfast

3 eggs +
spinach

🌮 Lunch

big veggie
salad

🍲 Dinner

chicken lettuce
wraps

🧁 Snack

apple + almond
butter

Water Intake

[■] [■] [■] [■] [ ] [ ] [ ] [ ] [ ]

Hunger Scale

1 2 3 4 ⑤ 6 7 8 9 10

starving   dinner   So Full

I Ate Because

☐ STARVING   ☐ CRAVINGS   ☒ TROUBLED   ☐ MOODY   ☐ NEED FUEL

Symptoms/Feelings Post Meal ➜ How Long After Meal?

☐ STRONG   ☒ BLOATING   ☐ DIGESTIVE   ☐ < 1HOUR   ☒ 1 - 2 HOURS

☐ FOCUSED   ☐ FOGGY MIND   ☐ OTHER

what? where? When? Why?

When I'm hungry, do I think about food repeatedly? when I feel
hungry before lunch, I think about eating frequently,
but before dinner, I don't think about eating much

Date: _____   Sleep Time: _____   😄 🙂 😐 ☹️ 😣

☕ Breakfast   🌮 Lunch   🍃 Dinner

_____   _____   _____
_____   _____   _____
_____   _____   _____
_____   _____   _____

🧁 Snack   Water Intake

_____   🥛 🥛 🥛 🥛 🥛 🥛 🥛 🥛 🥛
_____
                              Hunger Scale
_____
_____   1 2 3 4 5 6 7 8 9 10
                         starving   So Full

_____ I Ate Because _____

☐ STARVING   ☐ CRAVINGS   ☐ TROUBLED   ☐ MOODY   ☐ NEED FUEL

┌ Symptoms/Feelings Post Meal ──────▶ How Long After Meal? ┐

☐ STRONG   ☐ BLOATING   ☐ DIGESTIVE   ☐ < 1HOUR   ☐ 1 - 2 HOURS

☐ FOCUSED   ☐ FOGGY MIND   ☐ OTHER _____

what? where? When? Why?

When I'm hungry, do I think about food repeatedly? _____

_____
_____
_____
_____

Date: _____ Sleep Time: _____ 😁 🙂 😐 🙁 😣

☕ Breakfast   🌮 Lunch   🍽 Dinner

_____   _____   _____
_____   _____   _____
_____   _____   _____
_____   _____   _____
_____   _____   _____

🧁 Snack

_____   ──── Water Intake ────
_____   [ ] [ ] [ ] [ ] [ ] [ ] [ ] [ ] [ ]
_____
_____   ──── Hunger Scale ────
_____   1 2 3 4 5 6 7 8 9 10
                      starving   So Full

──── I Ate Because ────
[ ] STARVING   [ ] CRAVINGS   [ ] TROUBLED   [ ] MOODY   [ ] NEED FUEL

── Symptoms/Feelings Post Meal ──→ How Long After Meal? ──
[ ] STRONG   [ ] BLOATING   [ ] DIGESTIVE   [ ] < 1HOUR   [ ] 1 - 2 HOURS
[ ] FOCUSED   [ ] FOGGY MIND   [ ] OTHER _____

what? where? When? Why?

Am I afraid to lose control when I have dinner quickly? _____

_____
_____
_____
_____
_____

Date: _____ Sleep Time: _____ 😁 🙂 😐 ☹️ 😣

☕ Breakfast   🌮 Lunch   🍜 Dinner

_____ _____ _____

_____ _____ _____

_____ _____ _____

_____ _____ _____

_____ _____ _____

🧁 Snack

_____

_____

_____

_____

Water Intake

[ ] [ ] [ ] [ ] [ ] [ ] [ ] [ ] [ ]

Hunger Scale

1 2 3 4 5 6 7 8 9 10

starving   So Full

I Ate Because

[ ] STARVING [ ] CRAVINGS [ ] TROUBLED [ ] MOODY [ ] NEED FUEL

Symptoms/Feelings Post Meal ➡️ How Long After Meal?

[ ] STRONG [ ] BLOATING [ ] DIGESTIVE [ ] < 1HOUR [ ] 1 - 2 HOURS

[ ] FOCUSED [ ] FOGGY MIND [ ] OTHER _____

what? where? When? Why?

Which foods seem most appealing? How much of them would
I like to eat? _____

_____

_____

_____

_____

Date: _____   Sleep Time: _____   😄 🙂 😐 🙁 😣

☕ Breakfast   🌮 Lunch   🍝 Dinner

_____   _____   _____
_____   _____   _____
_____   _____   _____
_____   _____   _____
_____   _____   _____

🧁 Snack   ___ Water Intake ___

_____   [ ] [ ] [ ] [ ] [ ] [ ] [ ] [ ] [ ]
_____
_____   ___ Hunger Scale ___
_____
                           1 2 3 4 5 6 7 8 9 10
                           starving   So Full

─── I Ate Because ───
[ ] STARVING   [ ] CRAVINGS   [ ] TROUBLED   [ ] MOODY   [ ] NEED FUEL

─ Symptoms/Feelings Post Meal ──➤ How Long After Meal? ─
[ ] STRONG   [ ] BLOATING   [ ] DIGESTIVE   [ ] < 1HOUR   [ ] 1 - 2 HOURS
[ ] FOCUSED   [ ] FOGGY MIND [ ] OTHER _____

what? where? When? Why?

Bring your focus back to your body and your breathing. How do you feel?

_____
_____
_____
_____
_____

Date: _____ Sleep Time: _____ 😀 🙂 😐 ☹️ 😣

☕ Breakfast   🌮 Lunch   🍲 Dinner

_____   _____   _____
_____   _____   _____
_____   _____   _____
_____   _____   _____

🧁 Snack

_____

_____

_____

Water Intake

[glass] [glass] [glass] [glass] [glass] [glass] [glass] [glass] [glass]

Hunger Scale

1   2   3   4   5   6   7   8   9   10

starving   So Full

I Ate Because

☐ STARVING   ☐ CRAVINGS   ☐ TROUBLED   ☐ MOODY   ☐ NEED FUEL

Symptoms/Feelings Post Meal ➡️ How Long After Meal?

☐ STRONG   ☐ BLOATING   ☐ DIGESTIVE   ☐ < 1HOUR   ☐ 1 - 2 HOURS

☐ FOCUSED   ☐ FOGGY MIND   ☐ OTHER _____

what? where? When? Why?

Am I still hungry or thirsty? _____

_____

_____

_____

_____

Date: _____ Sleep Time: _____ 😄 🙂 😐 🙁 😣

☕ Breakfast   🌮 Lunch   🍽 Dinner

_____   _____   _____
_____   _____   _____
_____   _____   _____
_____   _____   _____
_____   _____   _____

🧁 Snack

_____

_____   ——— Water Intake ———

_____   [ ] [ ] [ ] [ ] [ ] [ ] [ ] [ ] [ ]

_____   ——— Hunger Scale ———

                     1 2 3 4 5 6 7 8 9 10
                     starving   So Full

——————————— I Ate Because ———————————

[ ] STARVING   [ ] CRAVINGS   [ ] TROUBLED   [ ] MOODY   [ ] NEED FUEL

— Symptoms/Feelings Post Meal ——→ How Long After Meal? —

[ ] STRONG   [ ] BLOATING   [ ] DIGESTIVE   [ ] < 1HOUR   [ ] 1 - 2 HOURS

[ ] FOCUSED   [ ] FOGGY MIND   [ ] OTHER _____

what? where? When? Why?

(Today) Do I really need to eat any more? _____

_____

_____

_____

_____

_____

Date: _____ Sleep Time: _____ 😁 🙂 😐 🙁 😫

☕ Breakfast

_____
_____
_____
_____

🌮 Lunch

_____
_____
_____
_____

🍝 Dinner

_____
_____
_____
_____

🧁 Snack

_____
_____
_____
_____

Water Intake

[ ] [ ] [ ] [ ] [ ] [ ] [ ] [ ] [ ]

Hunger Scale

1   2   3   4   5   6   7   8   9   10

starving   So Full

I Ate Because

☐ STARVING   ☐ CRAVINGS   ☐ TROUBLED   ☐ MOODY   ☐ NEED FUEL

Symptoms/Feelings Post Meal ➡ How Long After Meal?

☐ STRONG   ☐ BLOATING   ☐ DIGESTIVE   ☐ < 1HOUR   ☐ 1 - 2 HOURS

☐ FOCUSED   ☐ FOGGY MIND   ☐ OTHER _____

what? where? When? Why?

Where do I think My food comes from? _____

_____
_____
_____
_____

Date: _____ Sleep Time: _____ 😄 🙂 😐 🙁 😣

☕ Breakfast   🌮 Lunch   🍳 Dinner

_____   _____   _____
_____   _____   _____
_____   _____   _____
_____   _____   _____
_____   _____   _____

🧁 Snack

_____   ____ Water Intake ____
_____   [ ] [ ] [ ] [ ] [ ] [ ] [ ] [ ] [ ]
_____
_____   ____ Hunger Scale ____
_____   1 2 3 4 5 6 7 8 9 10
                      ├─────────────────────────
                      starving   So Full

_____ I Ate Because _____
☐ STARVING   ☐ CRAVINGS   ☐ TROUBLED   ☐ MOODY   ☐ NEED FUEL

┌ Symptoms/Feelings Post Meal ──────▶ How Long After Meal? ─┐
│ ☐ STRONG   ☐ BLOATING   ☐ DIGESTIVE   ☐ < 1HOUR   ☐ 1 - 2 HOURS │
│ ☐ FOCUSED ☐ FOGGY MIND ☐ OTHER _____ │
└──┘

what? where? When? Why?

How does my food grow, and what do I think it needs to help it grow?

_____
_____
_____
_____
_____

Date: _____ Sleep Time: _____ 😄 🙂 😐 ☹️ 😖

☕ Breakfast

_____
_____
_____
_____
_____

🌮 Lunch

_____
_____
_____
_____
_____

🍜 Dinner

_____
_____
_____
_____
_____

🧁 Snack

_____
_____
_____
_____

Water Intake

🥛 🥛 🥛 🥛 🥛 🥛 🥛 🥛 🥛

Hunger Scale

1 2 3 4 5 6 7 8 9 10

starving   So Full

I Ate Because

☐ STARVING   ☐ CRAVINGS   ☐ TROUBLED   ☐ MOODY   ☐ NEED FUEL

Symptoms/Feelings Post Meal ———➤ How Long After Meal?

☐ STRONG   ☐ BLOATING   ☐ DIGESTIVE   ☐ < 1HOUR   ☐ 1 - 2 HOURS

☐ FOCUSED   ☐ FOGGY MIND   ☐ OTHER _____

what? where? When? Why?

What exercises did I use and how well did they work? _____

_____
_____
_____
_____

Date: _____ Sleep Time: _____ 😄 🙂 😐 🙁 😣

☕ Breakfast   🌮 Lunch   🍳 Dinner

_____   _____   _____
_____   _____   _____
_____   _____   _____
_____   _____   _____

🧁 Snack

_____

_____

_____

_____

Water Intake

[ ] [ ] [ ] [ ] [ ] [ ] [ ] [ ] [ ]

Hunger Scale

1   2   3   4   5   6   7   8   9   10

starving   So Full

I Ate Because

[ ] STARVING   [ ] CRAVINGS   [ ] TROUBLED   [ ] MOODY   [ ] NEED FUEL

Symptoms/Feelings Post Meal ➞ How Long After Meal?

[ ] STRONG   [ ] BLOATING   [ ] DIGESTIVE   [ ] < 1HOUR   [ ] 1 - 2 HOURS

[ ] FOCUSED   [ ] FOGGY MIND   [ ] OTHER _____

what? where? When? Why?

If I were going to eat or drink something right now, what is my hungry for? What is it thirsty for? _____

_____

_____

_____

Date: _____ Sleep Time: _____ 😄 🙂 😐 🙁 😣

☕ Breakfast   🌮 Lunch   🍝 Dinner

_____   _____   _____
_____   _____   _____
_____   _____   _____
_____   _____   _____
_____   _____   _____

🧁 Snack

_____

_____   _____ Water Intake _____

_____   [▯ ▯ ▯ ▯ ▯ ▯ ▯ ▯ ▯]

_____   _____ Hunger Scale _____

                         1 2 3 4 5 6 7 8 9 10
                         |—————————————————————————|
                         starving   So Full

_____ I Ate Because _____

☐ STARVING   ☐ CRAVINGS   ☐ TROUBLED   ☐ MOODY   ☐ NEED FUEL

— Symptoms/Feelings Post Meal ——→ How Long After Meal? —

☐ STRONG   ☐ BLOATING   ☐ DIGESTIVE   ☐ < 1HOUR   ☐ 1 - 2 HOURS

☐ FOCUSED   ☐ FOGGY MIND   ☐ OTHER _____

what? where? When? Why?

When do I feel like eating? _____

_____
_____
_____
_____
_____

Date: _____ Sleep Time: _____ 😄 🙂 😐 🙁 😣

☕ Breakfast   🌮 Lunch   🍽 Dinner

_____   _____   _____

_____   _____   _____

_____   _____   _____

_____   _____   _____

🧁 Snack

_____

_____

_____

_____

Water Intake

[ ] [ ] [ ] [ ] [ ] [ ] [ ] [ ] [ ]

Hunger Scale

1 2 3 4 5 6 7 8 9 10

starving   So Full

I Ate Because

[ ] STARVING [ ] CRAVINGS [ ] TROUBLED [ ] MOODY [ ] NEED FUEL

Symptoms/Feelings Post Meal ⟶ How Long After Meal?

[ ] STRONG [ ] BLOATING [ ] DIGESTIVE [ ] < 1 HOUR [ ] 1 - 2 HOURS

[ ] FOCUSED [ ] FOGGY MIND [ ] OTHER _____

what? where? When? Why?

What is driving my eating at any given time? _____

_____

_____

_____

_____

_____

Date: _____ Sleep Time: _____ 😄 🙂 😐 🙁 😣

☕ Breakfast   🌮 Lunch   🍝 Dinner

_____   _____   _____
_____   _____   _____
_____   _____   _____
_____   _____   _____
_____   _____   _____

🧁 Snack

_____

_____   ___ Water Intake ___
                         [🥛 🥛 🥛 🥛 🥛 🥛 🥛 🥛 🥛]
_____

_____   ___ Hunger Scale ___
                         1 2 3 4 5 6 7 8 9 10
_____   starving   So Full

___ I Ate Because ___
☐ STARVING   ☐ CRAVINGS   ☐ TROUBLED   ☐ MOODY   ☐ NEED FUEL

— Symptoms/Feelings Post Meal ——▶ How Long After Meal? —
☐ STRONG   ☐ BLOATING   ☐ DIGESTIVE   ☐ < 1HOUR   ☐ 1 - 2 HOURS
☐ FOCUSED ☐ FOGGY MIND ☐ OTHER _____

what? where? When? Why?

How do I get the food I have chosen into my body? _____

_____
_____
_____
_____

Date: ____________ Sleep Time: ____________

Breakfast

Lunch

Dinner

Snack

Water Intake

Hunger Scale

1 2 3 4 5 6 7 8 9 10

starving So Full

I Ate Because

☐ STARVING ☐ CRAVINGS ☐ TROUBLED ☐ MOODY ☐ NEED FUEL

Symptoms/Feelings Post Meal → How Long After Meal?

☐ STRONG ☐ BLOATING ☐ DIGESTIVE ☐ < 1HOUR ☐ 1 - 2 HOURS

☐ FOCUSED ☐ FOGGY MIND ☐ OTHER ____________

what? where? When? Why?

How did I feel today before the meals? ____________

Date: _____ Sleep Time: _____ 😄 ☺ 😐 🙁 😣

☕ Breakfast

_____
_____
_____
_____
_____

🌮 Lunch

_____
_____
_____
_____
_____

🍝 Dinner

_____
_____
_____
_____
_____

🧁 Snack

_____
_____
_____
_____

Water Intake

🥛 🥛 🥛 🥛 🥛 🥛 🥛 🥛 🥛

Hunger Scale

1 2 3 4 5 6 7 8 9 10

starving   So Full

I Ate Because

☐ STARVING ☐ CRAVINGS ☐ TROUBLED ☐ MOODY ☐ NEED FUEL

Symptoms/Feelings Post Meal ⟶ How Long After Meal?

☐ STRONG ☐ BLOATING ☐ DIGESTIVE ☐ < 1HOUR ☐ 1 - 2 HOURS

☐ FOCUSED ☐ FOGGY MIND ☐ OTHER _____

what? where? When? Why?

can I describe the eating environment at work? _____

_____
_____
_____
_____

Date: _____ Sleep Time: _____ 😄 🙂 😐 🙁 😣

☕ Breakfast   🌮 Lunch   🍲 Dinner

_____   _____   _____
_____   _____   _____
_____   _____   _____
_____   _____   _____
_____   _____   _____

🧁 Snack

_____

Water Intake

[glass] [glass] [glass] [glass] [glass] [glass] [glass] [glass] [glass]

_____

Hunger Scale

1   2   3   4   5   6   7   8   9   10
starving   So Full

_____

I Ate Because

☐ STARVING   ☐ CRAVINGS   ☐ TROUBLED   ☐ MOODY   ☐ NEED FUEL

Symptoms/Feelings Post Meal ⟶ How Long After Meal?

☐ STRONG   ☐ BLOATING   ☐ DIGESTIVE   ☐ < 1HOUR   ☐ 1 - 2 HOURS

☐ FOCUSED   ☐ FOGGY MIND   ☐ OTHER _____

what? where? When? Why?

What are at four things I don't eat mindfully at lunch or when having
dinner? _____

- _____
- _____
- _____
- _____

Date: _____ Sleep Time: _____ 😄 ☺ 😐 ☹ 😣

☕ Breakfast

_____
_____
_____
_____
_____

🌮 Lunch

_____
_____
_____
_____
_____

🍝 Dinner

_____
_____
_____
_____
_____

🧁 Snack

_____
_____
_____
_____

Water Intake

[glass] [glass] [glass] [glass] [glass] [glass] [glass] [glass] [glass]

Hunger Scale

1   2   3   4   5   6   7   8   9   10

starving   So Full

I Ate Because

☐ STARVING   ☐ CRAVINGS   ☐ TROUBLED   ☐ MOODY   ☐ NEED FUEL

Symptoms/Feelings Post Meal ⟶ How Long After Meal?

☐ STRONG   ☐ BLOATING   ☐ DIGESTIVE   ☐ < 1HOUR   ☐ 1 - 2 HOURS

☐ FOCUSED   ☐ FOGGY MIND   ☐ OTHER _____

what? where? When? Why?

Where do I eat (at home)? _____
_____
_____
_____
_____

Date: _____ Sleep Time: _____ 😄 ☺ 😐 🙁 😣

☕ Breakfast

_____
_____
_____
_____
_____

🥪 Lunch

_____
_____
_____
_____
_____

🍽 Dinner

_____
_____
_____
_____
_____

🧁 Snack

_____
_____
_____
_____

——————— Water Intake ———————

🥛 🥛 🥛 🥛 🥛 🥛 🥛 🥛 🥛

——————— Hunger Scale ———————

1 2 3 4 5 6 7 8 9 10

starving   So Full

——————— I Ate Because ———————

☐ STARVING ☐ CRAVINGS ☐ TROUBLED ☐ MOODY ☐ NEED FUEL

— Symptoms/Feelings Post Meal ——➤ How Long After Meal? —

☐ STRONG ☐ BLOATING ☐ DIGESTIVE ☐ < 1HOUR ☐ 1 - 2 HOURS

☐ FOCUSED ☐ FOGGY MIND ☐ OTHER _____

what? where? When? Why?

Today while eating (lunch), Am I busy or calm? _____

_____
_____
_____
_____

Date: _____ Sleep Time: _____ 😄 🙂 😐 🙁 😣

☕ Breakfast   🌮 Lunch   🍝 Dinner

_____   _____   _____
_____   _____   _____
_____   _____   _____
_____   _____   _____
_____   _____   _____

🧁 Snack

_____

_____

_____

_____

Water Intake

🥛 🥛 🥛 🥛 🥛 🥛 🥛 🥛 🥛

Hunger Scale

1 2 3 4 5 6 7 8 9 10

starving   So Full

I Ate Because

☐ STARVING   ☐ CRAVINGS   ☐ TROUBLED   ☐ MOODY   ☐ NEED FUEL

Symptoms/Feelings Post Meal ➡️ How Long After Meal?

☐ STRONG   ☐ BLOATING   ☐ DIGESTIVE   ☐ < 1HOUR   ☐ 1 - 2 HOURS

☐ FOCUSED   ☐ FOGGY MIND   ☐ OTHER _____

what? where? When? Why?

What types of foods that I prevent myself from eating? _____

_____

_____

_____

_____

Date: _____ Sleep Time: _____ 😁 🙂 😐 🙁 😣

☕ Breakfast ⠀⠀⠀ 🌮 Lunch ⠀⠀⠀ 🍽 Dinner

_____ ⠀ _____ ⠀ _____
_____ ⠀ _____ ⠀ _____
_____ ⠀ _____ ⠀ _____
_____ ⠀ _____ ⠀ _____
_____ ⠀ _____ ⠀ _____

🧁 Snack

_____

_____ ⠀⠀⠀⠀⠀ Water Intake _____

_____

_____ ⠀⠀⠀⠀⠀ Hunger Scale _____

_____

⠀⠀⠀⠀⠀⠀⠀⠀⠀ 1 ⠀ 2 ⠀ 3 ⠀ 4 ⠀ 5 ⠀ 6 ⠀ 7 ⠀ 8 ⠀ 9 ⠀ 10
⠀⠀⠀⠀⠀⠀⠀⠀⠀ starving ⠀⠀⠀⠀⠀⠀⠀⠀⠀⠀⠀⠀⠀⠀⠀ So Full

_____ I Ate Because _____

☐ STARVING ⠀ ☐ CRAVINGS ⠀ ☐ TROUBLED ⠀ ☐ MOODY ⠀ ☐ NEED FUEL

_ Symptoms/Feelings Post Meal ⟶ How Long After Meal? _

☐ STRONG ⠀ ☐ BLOATING ⠀ ☐ DIGESTIVE ⠀ ☐ < 1HOUR ⠀ ☐ 1 - 2 HOURS

☐ FOCUSED ⠀ ☐ FOGGY MIND ⠀ ☐ OTHER _____

what? where? When? Why?

Do I feel guilty when I eat foods that I previously refrained from? _____

_____
_____
_____
_____

Date: _____ Sleep Time: _____ 😄 🙂 😐 🙁 😣

☕ Breakfast   🌮 Lunch   🍝 Dinner

_____   _____   _____
_____   _____   _____
_____   _____   _____
_____   _____   _____

🧁 Snack

_____
_____
_____
_____

Water Intake

🥛 🥛 🥛 🥛 🥛 🥛 🥛 🥛 🥛

Hunger Scale

1   2   3   4   5   6   7   8   9   10

starving   So Full

I Ate Because

☐ STARVING   ☐ CRAVINGS   ☐ TROUBLED   ☐ MOODY   ☐ NEED FUEL

Symptoms/Feelings Post Meal ➔ How Long After Meal?

☐ STRONG   ☐ BLOATING   ☐ DIGESTIVE   ☐ < 1HOUR   ☐ 1 - 2 HOURS

☐ FOCUSED   ☐ FOGGY MIND   ☐ OTHER _____

what? where? When? Why?

Am I afraid to lose control when I have lunch quickly? _____

_____
_____
_____
_____

Date: _____ Sleep Time: _____ 😄 ☺ 😐 ☹ 😖

☕ Breakfast

_____
_____
_____
_____
_____

🌮 Lunch

_____
_____
_____
_____
_____

🍂 Dinner

_____
_____
_____
_____
_____

🧁 Snack

_____
_____
_____
_____

Water Intake

🥛 🥛 🥛 🥛 🥛 🥛 🥛 🥛 🥛

Hunger Scale

1 2 3 4 5 6 7 8 9 10

starving   So Full

I Ate Because

☐ STARVING ☐ CRAVINGS ☐ TROUBLED ☐ MOODY ☐ NEED FUEL

Symptoms/Feelings Post Meal ➤ How Long After Meal?

☐ STRONG ☐ BLOATING ☐ DIGESTIVE ☐ < 1HOUR ☐ 1 - 2 HOURS

☐ FOCUSED ☐ FOGGY MIND ☐ OTHER _____

what? where? When? Why?

(At work)Do I eat fast, barely eating my food? why? _____

_____
_____
_____
_____

Date: _____ Sleep Time: _____ 😁 🙂 😐 🙁 😣

☕ Breakfast

_____
_____
_____
_____
_____

🌮 Lunch

_____
_____
_____
_____
_____

🍝 Dinner

_____
_____
_____
_____
_____

🧁 Snack

_____
_____
_____
_____

Water Intake

🥛 🥛 🥛 🥛 🥛 🥛 🥛 🥛 🥛

Hunger Scale

1 2 3 4 5 6 7 8 9 10

starving   So Full

I Ate Because

☐ STARVING ☐ CRAVINGS ☐ TROUBLED ☐ MOODY ☐ NEED FUEL

Symptoms/Feelings Post Meal ➡ How Long After Meal?

☐ STRONG   ☐ BLOATING   ☐ DIGESTIVE   ☐ < 1HOUR   ☐ 1 - 2 HOURS

☐ FOCUSED ☐ FOGGY MIND ☐ OTHER _____

what? where? When? Why?

What emotions trigger me to overeat? _____

_____
_____
_____
_____

Date: _____ Sleep Time: _____ 😁 ☺ 😐 ☹ 😣

☕ Breakfast   🌮 Lunch   🍽 Dinner

_____   _____   _____
_____   _____   _____
_____   _____   _____
_____   _____   _____
_____   _____   _____

🧁 Snack

_____

_____

_____

_____

Water Intake

🥛 🥛 🥛 🥛 🥛 🥛 🥛 🥛 🥛

Hunger Scale

1 2 3 4 5 6 7 8 9 10

starving   So Full

I Ate Because

☐ STARVING   ☐ CRAVINGS   ☐ TROUBLED   ☐ MOODY   ☐ NEED FUEL

Symptoms/Feelings Post Meal ➡ How Long After Meal?

☐ STRONG   ☐ BLOATING   ☐ DIGESTIVE   ☐ < 1HOUR   ☐ 1 - 2 HOURS

☐ FOCUSED   ☐ FOGGY MIND   ☐ OTHER _____

what? where? When? Why?

Do I have a plan to refrain from eating beside the computer or watching TV? What's the plan? _____

_____

_____

_____

Date:_____ Sleep Time: _____ 😁 🙂 😐 🙁 😣

☕ Breakfast   🌮 Lunch   🍝 Dinner

_____   _____   _____
_____   _____   _____
_____   _____   _____
_____   _____   _____
_____   _____   _____

🧁 Snack

_____   _____ Water Intake _____
                     ☐ ☐ ☐ ☐ ☐ ☐ ☐ ☐ ☐
_____

_____   _____ Hunger Scale _____
_____   1 2 3 4 5 6 7 8 9 10
_____ |———————————————————————|
_____   starving   So Full

_____ I Ate Because _____
☐ STARVING ☐ CRAVINGS ☐ TROUBLED ☐ MOODY ☐ NEED FUEL

_ Symptoms/Feelings Post Meal ——→ How Long After Meal? _
☐ STRONG   ☐ BLOATING   ☐ DIGESTIVE   ☐ < 1HOUR   ☐ 1 - 2 HOURS
☐ FOCUSED ☐ FOGGY MIND ☐ OTHER _____

what? where? When? Why?

Do I exercise? What exercises do I would prefer? _____

_____
_____
_____
_____
_____

Date: _____ Sleep Time: _____ 😁 🙂 😐 🙁 😣

☕ Breakfast   🌮 Lunch   🍃 Dinner

_____   _____   _____
_____   _____   _____
_____   _____   _____
_____   _____   _____
_____   _____   _____

🧁 Snack   Water Intake

_____   [ ] [ ] [ ] [ ] [ ] [ ] [ ] [ ] [ ]

_____   Hunger Scale

_____ | 1 2 3 4 5 6 7 8 9 10 |
                        | starving   So Full |
_____

──────────────── I Ate Because ────────────────
☐ STARVING   ☐ CRAVINGS   ☐ TROUBLED   ☐ MOODY   ☐ NEED FUEL

── Symptoms/Feelings Post Meal ──➤ How Long After Meal? ──
☐ STRONG   ☐ BLOATING   ☐ DIGESTIVE   ☐ < 1HOUR   ☐ 1 - 2 HOURS

☐ FOCUSED   ☐ FOGGY MIND ☐ OTHER _____

what? where? When? Why?

How many times a day do I feel so hungry? _____

_____

_____

_____

_____

Date: _____ Sleep Time: _____ 😄 🙂 😐 🙁 😖

☕ Breakfast

_____
_____
_____
_____
_____

🌮 Lunch

_____
_____
_____
_____
_____

🍃 Dinner

_____
_____
_____
_____
_____

🧁 Snack

_____
_____
_____
_____

Water Intake

🥛 🥛 🥛 🥛 🥛 🥛 🥛 🥛 🥛

Hunger Scale

1 2 3 4 5 6 7 8 9 10

starving   So Full

I Ate Because

☐ STARVING ☐ CRAVINGS ☐ TROUBLED ☐ MOODY ☐ NEED FUEL

Symptoms/Feelings Post Meal ➡ How Long After Meal?

☐ STRONG ☐ BLOATING ☐ DIGESTIVE ☐ < 1HOUR ☐ 1 - 2 HOURS

☐ FOCUSED ☐ FOGGY MIND ☐ OTHER _____

what? where? When? Why?

Did I try to cut out some meals during the day? _____

_____
_____
_____
_____

Date: _____ Sleep Time: _____ 😁 🙂 😐 🙁 😫

☕ Breakfast   🌮 Lunch   🍽 Dinner

_____   _____   _____
_____   _____   _____
_____   _____   _____
_____   _____   _____
_____   _____   _____

🧁 Snack

_____

_____   — Water Intake —
_____   [ ] [ ] [ ] [ ] [ ] [ ] [ ] [ ] [ ]
_____
_____   — Hunger Scale —
                      1 2 3 4 5 6 7 8 9 10
                      |———————————————————————|
                      starving   So Full

— I Ate Because —
[ ] STARVING   [ ] CRAVINGS   [ ] TROUBLED   [ ] MOODY   [ ] NEED FUEL

— Symptoms/Feelings Post Meal ——→ How Long After Meal? —
[ ] STRONG   [ ] BLOATING   [ ] DIGESTIVE   [ ] < 1HOUR   [ ] 1 - 2 HOURS
[ ] FOCUSED   [ ] FOGGY MIND   [ ] OTHER

what? where? When? Why?

Write down health problems you can have while eating certain foods

- _____
- _____
- _____
- _____
- _____

Date: _____   Sleep Time: _____   😄 🙂 😐 🙁 😣

☕ Breakfast

_____
_____
_____
_____
_____

🌮 Lunch

_____
_____
_____
_____
_____

🍤 Dinner

_____
_____
_____
_____
_____

🧁 Snack

_____
_____
_____
_____

Water Intake

🥛 🥛 🥛 🥛 🥛 🥛 🥛 🥛 🥛

Hunger Scale

1   2   3   4   5   6   7   8   9   10

starving   So Full

I Ate Because

☐ STARVING   ☐ CRAVINGS   ☐ TROUBLED   ☐ MOODY   ☐ NEED FUEL

Symptoms/Feelings Post Meal ➝ How Long After Meal?

☐ STRONG   ☐ BLOATING   ☐ DIGESTIVE   ☐ < 1HOUR   ☐ 1 - 2 HOURS

☐ FOCUSED   ☐ FOGGY MIND   ☐ OTHER _____

what? where? When? Why?

What are four healthy foods that help me feel better? _____

_____
_____
_____
_____
_____

Date: _____ Sleep Time: _____ 😄 🙂 😐 🙁 😣

☕ Breakfast   🌮 Lunch   🍝 Dinner

_____   _____   _____
_____   _____   _____
_____   _____   _____
_____   _____   _____
_____   _____   _____

🧁 Snack

_____

Water Intake

[glass] [glass] [glass] [glass] [glass] [glass] [glass] [glass] [glass]

_____

Hunger Scale

1   2   3   4   5   6   7   8   9   10

starving   So Full

_____

I Ate Because

☐ STARVING ☐ CRAVINGS ☐ TROUBLED ☐ MOODY ☐ NEED FUEL

Symptoms/Feelings Post Meal ⟶ How Long After Meal?

☐ STRONG   ☐ BLOATING   ☐ DIGESTIVE   ☐ < 1HOUR   ☐ 1 - 2 HOURS
☐ FOCUSED   ☐ FOGGY MIND ☐ OTHER _____

what? where? When? Why?

What specific change would I make to improve my diet? _____

_____
_____
_____
_____

Date: _____ Sleep Time: _____ 😁 🙂 😐 🙁 😫

☕ Breakfast

_____
_____
_____
_____
_____

🌮 Lunch

_____
_____
_____
_____
_____

🍲 Dinner

_____
_____
_____
_____
_____

🧁 Snack

_____
_____
_____
_____

Water Intake

🥛 🥛 🥛 🥛 🥛 🥛 🥛 🥛 🥛

Hunger Scale

1   2   3   4   5   6   7   8   9   10

starving   So Full

I Ate Because

☐ STARVING   ☐ CRAVINGS   ☐ TROUBLED   ☐ MOODY   ☐ NEED FUEL

Symptoms/Feelings Post Meal ➔ How Long After Meal?

☐ STRONG   ☐ BLOATING   ☐ DIGESTIVE   ☐ < 1HOUR   ☐ 1 - 2 HOURS

☐ FOCUSED   ☐ FOGGY MIND   ☐ OTHER _____

what? where? When? Why?

What emotions trigger me to not overeat? _____

_____
_____
_____
_____

Date: _____ Sleep Time: _____ 😁 🙂 😐 🙁 😣

☕ Breakfast

_____
_____
_____
_____
_____

🌮 Lunch

_____
_____
_____
_____
_____

🍝 Dinner

_____
_____
_____
_____
_____

🧁 Snack

_____
_____
_____
_____

Water Intake

🥛 🥛 🥛 🥛 🥛 🥛 🥛 🥛 🥛

Hunger Scale

1 2 3 4 5 6 7 8 9 10

starving   So Full

I Ate Because

☐ STARVING ☐ CRAVINGS ☐ TROUBLED ☐ MOODY ☐ NEED FUEL

Symptoms/Feelings Post Meal ➡ How Long After Meal?

☐ STRONG ☐ BLOATING ☐ DIGESTIVE ☐ < 1HOUR ☐ 1 - 2 HOURS

☐ FOCUSED ☐ FOGGY MIND ☐ OTHER _____

what? where? When? Why?

When was the last time I feel painfully hungry (nausea, stomach upset, etc.)?

_____
_____
_____
_____
_____

Date: _____ Sleep Time: _____ 😄 ☺ 😐 ☹ 😣

☕ Breakfast   🌮 Lunch   🍜 Dinner

_____   _____   _____
_____   _____   _____
_____   _____   _____
_____   _____   _____
_____   _____   _____

🧁 Snack

_____

Water Intake

[glass] [glass] [glass] [glass] [glass] [glass] [glass] [glass] [glass]

_____

Hunger Scale

1   2   3   4   5   6   7   8   9   10
starving   So Full

_____

I Ate Because

☐ STARVING   ☐ CRAVINGS   ☐ TROUBLED   ☐ MOODY   ☐ NEED FUEL

Symptoms/Feelings Post Meal ➔ How Long After Meal?

☐ STRONG   ☐ BLOATING   ☐ DIGESTIVE   ☐ < 1HOUR   ☐ 1 - 2 HOURS

☐ FOCUSED   ☐ FOGGY MIND ☐ OTHER _____

what? where? When? Why?

How much fuel do I consume? _____

_____
_____
_____
_____
_____

Date: _____ Sleep Time: _____ 😄 🙂 😐 🙁 😣

☕ Breakfast

_____
_____
_____
_____
_____

🌮 Lunch

_____
_____
_____
_____
_____

🍽 Dinner

_____
_____
_____
_____
_____

🧁 Snack

_____
_____
_____
_____

Water Intake

🥛 🥛 🥛 🥛 🥛 🥛 🥛 🥛 🥛

Hunger Scale

1 2 3 4 5 6 7 8 9 10

starving   So Full

I Ate Because

☐ STARVING ☐ CRAVINGS ☐ TROUBLED ☐ MOODY ☐ NEED FUEL

Symptoms/Feelings Post Meal ⟶ How Long After Meal?

☐ STRONG ☐ BLOATING ☐ DIGESTIVE ☐ < 1HOUR ☐ 1 - 2 HOURS

☐ FOCUSED ☐ FOGGY MIND ☐ OTHER _____

what? where? When? Why?

Where do I invest the energy I consume? _____

_____
_____
_____
_____
_____

Date: _____ Sleep Time: _____ 😄 🙂 😐 ☹️ 😣

☕ Breakfast

_____
_____
_____
_____
_____

🌮 Lunch

_____
_____
_____
_____
_____

🍝 Dinner

_____
_____
_____
_____
_____

🧁 Snack

_____
_____
_____
_____

Water Intake

🥛 🥛 🥛 🥛 🥛 🥛 🥛 🥛 🥛

Hunger Scale

1 2 3 4 5 6 7 8 9 10

starving   So Full

I Ate Because

☐ STARVING   ☐ CRAVINGS   ☐ TROUBLED   ☐ MOODY   ☐ NEED FUEL

Symptoms/Feelings Post Meal ➔ How Long After Meal?

☐ STRONG   ☐ BLOATING   ☐ DIGESTIVE   ☐ < 1HOUR   ☐ 1 - 2 HOURS

☐ FOCUSED   ☐ FOGGY MIND   ☐ OTHER _____

what? where? When? Why?

How did I feel today after the meals? _____

_____
_____
_____
_____

Date: _____ Sleep Time: _____ 😄 🙂 😐 🙁 😣

☕ Breakfast

_____
_____
_____
_____
_____

🌮 Lunch

_____
_____
_____
_____
_____

🍳 Dinner

_____
_____
_____
_____
_____

🧁 Snack

_____
_____
_____
_____

Water Intake

🥛 🥛 🥛 🥛 🥛 🥛 🥛 🥛 🥛

Hunger Scale

| 1 | 2 | 3 | 4 | 5 | 6 | 7 | 8 | 9 | 10 |

starving | | | | | | | | | So Full

I Ate Because

☐ STARVING ☐ CRAVINGS ☐ TROUBLED ☐ MOODY ☐ NEED FUEL

Symptoms/Feelings Post Meal ➡ How Long After Meal?

☐ STRONG ☐ BLOATING ☐ DIGESTIVE ☐ < 1HOUR ☐ 1 - 2 HOURS

☐ FOCUSED ☐ FOGGY MIND ☐ OTHER _____

what? where? When? Why?

Today while eating (breakfast), Am I busy or calm? _____

_____
_____
_____
_____

Date: _____ Sleep Time: _____ 😄 🙂 😐 🙁 😣

☕ Breakfast   🌮 Lunch   🍝 Dinner

_____   _____   _____
_____   _____   _____
_____   _____   _____
_____   _____   _____

🧁 Snack

_____

_____

_____

_____

Water Intake

[🥛] [🥛] [🥛] [🥛] [🥛] [🥛] [🥛] [🥛] [🥛]

Hunger Scale

1 2 3 4 5 6 7 8 9 10

starving   So Full

I Ate Because

☐ STARVING   ☐ CRAVINGS   ☐ TROUBLED   ☐ MOODY   ☐ NEED FUEL

Symptoms/Feelings Post Meal ➜ How Long After Meal?

☐ STRONG   ☐ BLOATING   ☐ DIGESTIVE   ☐ < 1HOUR   ☐ 1 - 2 HOURS

☐ FOCUSED   ☐ FOGGY MIND ☐ OTHER _____

what? where? When? Why?

When was the last time I was extremely uncomfortably full to the point of nausea feeling sick? _____

_____

_____

_____

Date: _____ Sleep Time: _____ 😁 🙂 😐 🙁 😣

☕ Breakfast   🌮 Lunch   🍝 Dinner

_____   _____   _____
_____   _____   _____
_____   _____   _____
_____   _____   _____
_____   _____   _____

🧁 Snack

_____

_____

_____

_____

Water Intake

[glass][glass][glass][glass][glass][glass][glass][glass][glass]

Hunger Scale

1   2   3   4   5   6   7   8   9   10

starving   So Full

I Ate Because

☐ STARVING   ☐ CRAVINGS   ☐ TROUBLED   ☐ MOODY   ☐ NEED FUEL

Symptoms/Feelings Post Meal ⟶ How Long After Meal?

☐ STRONG   ☐ BLOATING   ☐ DIGESTIVE   ☐ < 1HOUR   ☐ 1 - 2 HOURS

☐ FOCUSED   ☐ FOGGY MIND   ☐ OTHER _____

what? where? When? Why?

(While Eating) Anytime the stomach feels a little full but not completely satisfied? _____

_____

_____

_____

_____

Date: _____ Sleep Time: _____ 😄 🙂 😐 🙁 😣

☕ Breakfast   🌮 Lunch   🍝 Dinner

_____   _____   _____
_____   _____   _____
_____   _____   _____
_____   _____   _____
_____   _____   _____

🧁 Snack

_____   ____ Water Intake ____

_____   [glass][glass][glass][glass][glass][glass][glass][glass][glass]

_____   ____ Hunger Scale ____

_____   1   2   3   4   5   6   7   8   9   10
                     |—————————————————————————————————|
                     starving   So Full

____ I Ate Because ____

☐ STARVING   ☐ CRAVINGS   ☐ TROUBLED   ☐ MOODY   ☐ NEED FUEL

— Symptoms/Feelings Post Meal ——→ How Long After Meal? —

☐ STRONG   ☐ BLOATING   ☐ DIGESTIVE   ☐ < 1HOUR   ☐ 1 - 2 HOURS

☐ FOCUSED   ☐ FOGGY MIND   ☐ OTHER _____

what? where? When? Why?

When I'm hungry, Do I have trouble concentrating? _____

_____

_____

_____

_____

Date: _____ Sleep Time: _____ 😁 🙂 😐 🙁 😣

☕ Breakfast   🌮 Lunch   🍃 Dinner

_____   _____   _____
_____   _____   _____
_____   _____   _____
_____   _____   _____
_____   _____   _____

🧁 Snack

_____

_____

_____

_____

—— Water Intake ——
[glass] [glass] [glass] [glass] [glass] [glass] [glass] [glass] [glass]

—— Hunger Scale ——
1 2 3 4 5 6 7 8 9 10
starving   So Full

—— I Ate Because ——
☐ STARVING ☐ CRAVINGS ☐ TROUBLED ☐ MOODY ☐ NEED FUEL

— Symptoms/Feelings Post Meal ——➤ How Long After Meal? —
☐ STRONG   ☐ BLOATING   ☐ DIGESTIVE   ☐ < 1HOUR   ☐ 1 - 2 HOURS
☐ FOCUSED ☐ FOGGY MIND ☐ OTHER _____

what? where? When? Why?

How do I protect myself from the influence of food that can deplete
my energy (high sugar food, Greasy food, Etc)? _____

_____

_____

_____

Date: _____ Sleep Time: _____ 😄 🙂 😐 🙁 😣

☕ Breakfast   🌮 Lunch   🍝 Dinner

_____   _____   _____
_____   _____   _____
_____   _____   _____
_____   _____   _____

🧁 Snack   _____ Water Intake _____

_____   🥛 🥛 🥛 🥛 🥛 🥛 🥛 🥛 🥛
_____
_____   _____ Hunger Scale _____
_____
                          1 2 3 4 5 6 7 8 9 10
                          starving   So Full

_____ I Ate Because _____

☐ STARVING ☐ CRAVINGS ☐ TROUBLED ☐ MOODY ☐ NEED FUEL

— Symptoms/Feelings Post Meal ——→ How Long After Meal? —

☐ STRONG   ☐ BLOATING   ☐ DIGESTIVE   ☐ < 1HOUR ☐ 1 - 2 HOURS

☐ FOCUSED   ☐ FOGGY MIND ☐ OTHER _____

what? where? When? Why?

What are at four things I don't eat mindfully at breakfast or when having
a snack? _____

- _____
- _____
- _____
- _____

Date: _____ Sleep Time: _____ 😄 ☺ 😐 ☹ 😣

☕ Breakfast   🌮 Lunch   🍝 Dinner

_____   _____   _____
_____   _____   _____
_____   _____   _____
_____   _____   _____
_____   _____   _____

🧁 Snack

_____

_____

_____

_____

_____ Water Intake _____

[🥛 🥛 🥛 🥛 🥛 🥛 🥛 🥛 🥛]

_____ Hunger Scale _____

1   2   3   4   5   6   7   8   9   10
starving   So Full

_____ I Ate Because _____

☐ STARVING   ☐ CRAVINGS   ☐ TROUBLED   ☐ MOODY   ☐ NEED FUEL

— Symptoms/Feelings Post Meal ——→ How Long After Meal? —

☐ STRONG   ☐ BLOATING   ☐ DIGESTIVE   ☐ < 1HOUR   ☐ 1 - 2 HOURS

☐ FOCUSED   ☐ FOGGY MIND   ☐ OTHER _____

what? where? When? Why?

What scares me (about my health)? _____

_____

_____

_____

_____

_____

Date: _____   Sleep Time: _____   😁 🙂 😐 🙁 😣

☕ Breakfast   🌮 Lunch   🍜 Dinner

_____   _____   _____
_____   _____   _____
_____   _____   _____
_____   _____   _____
_____   _____   _____

🧁 Snack   ———— Water Intake ————

_____   [glass] [glass] [glass] [glass] [glass] [glass] [glass] [glass] [glass]
_____
_____   ———— Hunger Scale ————
_____
_____   1   2   3   4   5   6   7   8   9   10
                            starving   So Full

———— I Ate Because ————

☐ STARVING   ☐ CRAVINGS   ☐ TROUBLED   ☐ MOODY   ☐ NEED FUEL

— Symptoms/Feelings Post Meal ——→ How Long After Meal? —

☐ STRONG   ☐ BLOATING   ☐ DIGESTIVE   ☐ < 1HOUR   ☐ 1 - 2 HOURS

☐ FOCUSED   ☐ FOGGY MIND   ☐ OTHER _____

what? where? When? Why?

If there are any negative consequences, or fears, related to achieving
a healthy diet, what would it be? _____

_____

_____

_____

_____

Date: _____ Sleep Time: _____ 😄 🙂 😐 🙁 😣

☕ Breakfast   🌮 Lunch   🍝 Dinner

_____   _____   _____
_____   _____   _____
_____   _____   _____
_____   _____   _____
_____   _____   _____

🧁 Snack

_____

_____

_____

_____

Water Intake

[ ] [ ] [ ] [ ] [ ] [ ] [ ] [ ] [ ]

Hunger Scale

1 2 3 4 5 6 7 8 9 10

starving   So Full

I Ate Because

☐ STARVING   ☐ CRAVINGS   ☐ TROUBLED   ☐ MOODY   ☐ NEED FUEL

Symptoms/Feelings Post Meal ➜ How Long After Meal?

☐ STRONG   ☐ BLOATING   ☐ DIGESTIVE   ☐ < 1HOUR   ☐ 1 - 2 HOURS

☐ FOCUSED   ☐ FOGGY MIND   ☐ OTHER _____

what? where? When? Why?

What single and achievable commitment can I make to improve
my self-care? _____

_____

_____

_____

_____

Date: _____ Sleep Time: _____ 😁 🙂 😐 🙁 😖

☕ Breakfast   🌮 Lunch   🍜 Dinner

_____   _____   _____
_____   _____   _____
_____   _____   _____
_____   _____   _____
_____   _____   _____

🧁 Snack   Water Intake
                        ⎕ ⎕ ⎕ ⎕ ⎕ ⎕ ⎕ ⎕ ⎕
_____
                                Hunger Scale
_____   1 2 3 4 5 6 7 8 9 10
                        ├─────────────────────────┤
_____   starving   So Full

_____

─────────── I Ate Because ───────────
☐ STARVING   ☐ CRAVINGS   ☐ TROUBLED   ☐ MOODY   ☐ NEED FUEL

─ Symptoms/Feelings Post Meal ──→ How Long After Meal? ─
☐ STRONG   ☐ BLOATING   ☐ DIGESTIVE   ☐ < 1HOUR   ☐ 1 - 2 HOURS
☐ FOCUSED   ☐ FOGGY MIND ☐ OTHER _____

what? where? When? Why?

When I feel pain emotional - the best thing I can do for myself : _____

_____
_____
_____
_____

Date: _____ Sleep Time: _____ 😄 🙂 😐 🙁 😣

☕ Breakfast   🌮 Lunch   🍃 Dinner

_____ _____ _____
_____ _____ _____
_____ _____ _____
_____ _____ _____
_____ _____ _____

🧁 Snack

_____

___ Water Intake ___

[ ][ ][ ][ ][ ][ ][ ][ ][ ]

_____

___ Hunger Scale ___

1 2 3 4 5 6 7 8 9 10

starving   So Full

_____

———— I Ate Because ————

☐ STARVING ☐ CRAVINGS ☐ TROUBLED ☐ MOODY ☐ NEED FUEL

┌ Symptoms/Feelings Post Meal ——➤ How Long After Meal? ┐

☐ STRONG ☐ BLOATING ☐ DIGESTIVE ☐ < 1HOUR ☐ 1 - 2 HOURS

☐ FOCUSED ☐ FOGGY MIND ☐ OTHER _____

what? where? When? Why?

List the questions you need to answer urgently : _____

- _____
- _____
- _____
- _____
- _____

Date: _____ Sleep Time: _____ 😄 🙂 😐 ☹️ 😣

☕ Breakfast   🌮 Lunch   🍜 Dinner

_____   _____   _____
_____   _____   _____
_____   _____   _____
_____   _____   _____

🧁 Snack

_____

_____   ___ Water Intake ___

_____   ▯ ▯ ▯ ▯ ▯ ▯ ▯ ▯ ▯

_____   ___ Hunger Scale ___

                      1 2 3 4 5 6 7 8 9 10
                      ├─────────────────────────┤
                      starving   So Full

_____ I Ate Because _____

☐ STARVING   ☐ CRAVINGS   ☐ TROUBLED   ☐ MOODY   ☐ NEED FUEL

― Symptoms/Feelings Post Meal ──────▶ How Long After Meal? ―

☐ STRONG   ☐ BLOATING   ☐ DIGESTIVE   ☐ < 1HOUR   ☐ 1 - 2 HOURS

☐ FOCUSED   ☐ FOGGY MIND ☐ OTHER _____

what? where? When? Why?

How do I hesitate to take action on what I can eat? _____

_____

_____

_____

_____

Date: _____ Sleep Time: _____ 😁 🙂 😐 ☹️ 😣

☕ Breakfast   🌮 Lunch   🍽️ Dinner

_____   _____   _____
_____   _____   _____
_____   _____   _____
_____   _____   _____
_____   _____   _____

🧁 Snack

_____

Water Intake

_____

Hunger Scale

1 2 3 4 5 6 7 8 9 10

starving   So Full

I Ate Because

☐ STARVING   ☐ CRAVINGS   ☐ TROUBLED   ☐ MOODY   ☐ NEED FUEL

Symptoms/Feelings Post Meal ——→ How Long After Meal?

☐ STRONG   ☐ BLOATING   ☐ DIGESTIVE   ☐ < 1HOUR   ☐ 1 - 2 HOURS

☐ FOCUSED   ☐ FOGGY MIND ☐ OTHER _____

what? where? When? Why?

What are the foods I don't eat mindfully at lunch (at work)? _____

_____

_____

_____

_____

Date: _____ Sleep Time: _____ 😄 🙂 😐 🙁 😖

Breakfast
_____
_____
_____
_____
_____

Lunch
_____
_____
_____
_____
_____

Dinner
_____
_____
_____
_____
_____

Snack
_____
_____
_____
_____

Water Intake

Hunger Scale

1	2	3	4	5	6	7	8	9	10
starving									So Full

I Ate Because

☐ STARVING   ☐ CRAVINGS   ☐ TROUBLED   ☐ MOODY   ☐ NEED FUEL

Symptoms/Feelings Post Meal ⟶ How Long After Meal?

☐ STRONG   ☐ BLOATING   ☐ DIGESTIVE   ☐ < 1HOUR   ☐ 1 - 2 HOURS

☐ FOCUSED   ☐ FOGGY MIND   ☐ OTHER _____

what? where? When? Why?

What five things would I like to change most about myself ? _____

- _____
- _____
- _____
- _____
- _____

Date: _____ Sleep Time: _____ 😁 🙂 😐 🙁 😣

☕ Breakfast   🌮 Lunch   🍽 Dinner

_____   _____   _____
_____   _____   _____
_____   _____   _____
_____   _____   _____
_____   _____   _____

🧁 Snack

_____

_____

_____

_____

Water Intake

Hunger Scale

1   2   3   4   5   6   7   8   9   10

starving   So Full

I Ate Because

☐ STARVING   ☐ CRAVINGS   ☐ TROUBLED   ☐ MOODY   ☐ NEED FUEL

Symptoms/Feelings Post Meal ➡ How Long After Meal?

☐ STRONG   ☐ BLOATING   ☐ DIGESTIVE   ☐ < 1HOUR   ☐ 1 - 2 HOURS

☐ FOCUSED   ☐ FOGGY MIND   ☐ OTHER _____

what? where? When? Why?

If my body could speak, he would say : _____

_____

_____

_____

_____

_____

Date: _____ Sleep Time: _____ 😁 🙂 😐 🙁 😣

☕ Breakfast

_____
_____
_____
_____
_____

🌮 Lunch

_____
_____
_____
_____

🍝 Dinner

_____
_____
_____
_____

🧁 Snack

_____
_____
_____
_____

Water Intake

🥛 🥛 🥛 🥛 🥛 🥛 🥛 🥛 🥛

Hunger Scale

1　2　3　4　5　6　7　8　9　10

starving　　　　　　　　　　So Full

I Ate Because

☐ STARVING　☐ CRAVINGS　☐ TROUBLED　☐ MOODY　☐ NEED FUEL

Symptoms/Feelings Post Meal ➤ **How Long After Meal?**

☐ STRONG　☐ BLOATING　☐ DIGESTIVE　☐ < 1HOUR　☐ 1 - 2 HOURS

☐ FOCUSED　☐ FOGGY MIND　☐ OTHER _____

what? where? When? Why?

If I can change one thing in my diet, what should I change and why ?

_____
_____
_____
_____

Date: _____ Sleep Time: _____ 😁 🙂 😐 ☹️ 😣

☕ Breakfast 🌮 Lunch 🍃 Dinner

_____ _____ _____

_____ _____ _____

_____ _____ _____

_____ _____ _____

_____ _____ _____

🧁 Snack

_____

_____

_____

_____

Water Intake

[glass] [glass] [glass] [glass] [glass] [glass] [glass] [glass] [glass]

Hunger Scale

1 2 3 4 5 6 7 8 9 10

starving   So Full

I Ate Because

☐ STARVING ☐ CRAVINGS ☐ TROUBLED ☐ MOODY ☐ NEED FUEL

Symptoms/Feelings Post Meal ⟶ How Long After Meal?

☐ STRONG ☐ BLOATING ☐ DIGESTIVE ☐ < 1HOUR ☐ 1 - 2 HOURS

☐ FOCUSED ☐ FOGGY MIND ☐ OTHER _____

what? where? When? Why?

What are my favorite ways to take care of myself physically
and emotionally? _____

_____

_____

_____

Date: _____ Sleep Time: _____ 😄 🙂 😐 🙁 😖

☕ Breakfast   🌮 Lunch   🍝 Dinner

_____   _____   _____
_____   _____   _____
_____   _____   _____
_____   _____   _____
_____   _____   _____

🧁 Snack

_____

_____ Water Intake _____

🥛 🥛 🥛 🥛 🥛 🥛 🥛 🥛 🥛

_____

_____ Hunger Scale _____

1   2   3   4   5   6   7   8   9   10

starving   So Full

_____

_____ I Ate Because _____

☐ STARVING ☐ CRAVINGS ☐ TROUBLED ☐ MOODY ☐ NEED FUEL

— Symptoms/Feelings Post Meal ⟶ How Long After Meal? —

☐ STRONG ☐ BLOATING ☐ DIGESTIVE   ☐ < 1HOUR ☐ 1 - 2 HOURS

☐ FOCUSED ☐ FOGGY MIND ☐ OTHER _____

what? where? When? Why?

Am I ready to leave eating (high-sugar food, fatty food, etc.)? _____

_____
_____
_____
_____

Date: _____   Sleep Time: _____   😄 🙂 😐 🙁 😫

☕ Breakfast   🌮 Lunch   🍝 Dinner

_____   _____   _____
_____   _____   _____
_____   _____   _____
_____   _____   _____
_____   _____   _____

🧁 Snack

_____   _____ Water Intake _____
_____ | 🥛 🥛 🥛 🥛 🥛 🥛 🥛 🥛 🥛 |
_____
_____   _____ Hunger Scale _____
                     | 1 2 3 4 5 6 7 8 9 10 |
                     | starving   So Full |

_____ I Ate Because _____
☐ STARVING ☐ CRAVINGS ☐ TROUBLED ☐ MOODY ☐ NEED FUEL

— Symptoms/Feelings Post Meal ——➤ How Long After Meal? —
☐ STRONG   ☐ BLOATING   ☐ DIGESTIVE   ☐ < 1HOUR   ☐ 1 - 2 HOURS
☐ FOCUSED   ☐ FOGGY MIND   ☐ OTHER _____

what? where? When? Why?

How do I feel responsible for my health? _____

_____
_____
_____
_____

Date: _____ Sleep Time: _____ 😁 🙂 😐 ☹️ 😣

☕ Breakfast   🌮 Lunch   🍲 Dinner

_____ _____ _____
_____ _____ _____
_____ _____ _____
_____ _____ _____
_____ _____ _____

🧁 Snack

_____

_____

_____

_____

Water Intake

[ ] [ ] [ ] [ ] [ ] [ ] [ ] [ ] [ ]

Hunger Scale

1 2 3 4 5 6 7 8 9 10

starving   So Full

I Ate Because

☐ STARVING ☐ CRAVINGS ☐ TROUBLED ☐ MOODY ☐ NEED FUEL

Symptoms/Feelings Post Meal ⟶ How Long After Meal?

☐ STRONG ☐ BLOATING ☐ DIGESTIVE ☐ < 1HOUR ☐ 1 - 2 HOURS

☐ FOCUSED ☐ FOGGY MIND ☐ OTHER _____

what? where? When? Why?

If I have extra weight, what are the five things that cause that ? _____

- _____
- _____
- _____
- _____
- _____

Date: _____   Sleep Time: _____   😄 ☺ 😐 🙁 😣

☕ Breakfast   🌮 Lunch   🍲 Dinner

_____   _____   _____
_____   _____   _____
_____   _____   _____
_____   _____   _____
_____   _____   _____

🧁 Snack

_____   ___ Water Intake ___
_____   [glass][glass][glass][glass][glass][glass][glass][glass][glass]
_____
_____   ___ Hunger Scale ___
_____   1   2   3   4   5   6   7   8   9   10
                       starving   So Full

─── I Ate Because ───
☐ STARVING   ☐ CRAVINGS   ☐ TROUBLED   ☐ MOODY   ☐ NEED FUEL

┌─ Symptoms/Feelings Post Meal ──────▶ How Long After Meal? ─┐
☐ STRONG   ☐ BLOATING   ☐ DIGESTIVE   ☐ < 1HOUR   ☐ 1 - 2 HOURS
☐ FOCUSED   ☐ FOGGY MIND   ☐ OTHER _____

what? where? When? Why?

On a scale of 1 to 10, where am I when it comes to being calm and focused
in difficult situations ? _____

_____
_____
_____

Date: _____ Sleep Time: _____ 😄 🙂 😐 🙁 😣

☕ Breakfast   🌮 Lunch   🍝 Dinner

_____   _____   _____
_____   _____   _____
_____   _____   _____
_____   _____   _____
_____   _____   _____

🧁 Snack

_____

_____

_____

_____

Water Intake

[🥛] [🥛] [🥛] [🥛] [🥛] [🥛] [🥛] [🥛] [🥛]

Hunger Scale

1   2   3   4   5   6   7   8   9   10

starving   So Full

I Ate Because

☐ STARVING   ☐ CRAVINGS   ☐ TROUBLED   ☐ MOODY   ☐ NEED FUEL

Symptoms/Feelings Post Meal ➔ How Long After Meal?

☐ STRONG   ☐ BLOATING   ☐ DIGESTIVE   ☐ < 1HOUR   ☐ 1 - 2 HOURS

☐ FOCUSED   ☐ FOGGY MIND   ☐ OTHER _____

what? where? When? Why?

What prevents me from giving up unhealthy food ? _____

_____

_____

_____

_____

Date: _____ Sleep Time: _____ 😄 🙂 😐 🙁 😣

☕ Breakfast

_____
_____
_____
_____
_____

🌮 Lunch

_____
_____
_____
_____
_____

🍳 Dinner

_____
_____
_____
_____
_____

🧁 Snack

_____
_____
_____
_____

Water Intake

🥛 🥛 🥛 🥛 🥛 🥛 🥛 🥛 🥛

Hunger Scale

1 2 3 4 5 6 7 8 9 10

starving   So Full

I Ate Because

☐ STARVING ☐ CRAVINGS ☐ TROUBLED ☐ MOODY ☐ NEED FUEL

Symptoms/Feelings Post Meal ⟶ How Long After Meal?

☐ STRONG ☐ BLOATING ☐ DIGESTIVE ☐ < 1HOUR ☐ 1 - 2 HOURS

☐ FOCUSED ☐ FOGGY MIND ☐ OTHER _____

what? where? When? Why?

What is the foods that makes me wake up at night?_____

_____
_____
_____
_____

Date: _____ Sleep Time: _____ 😄 🙂 😐 🙁 😖

☕ Breakfast

_____
_____
_____
_____
_____

🌮 Lunch

_____
_____
_____
_____
_____

🍝 Dinner

_____
_____
_____
_____
_____

🧁 Snack

_____
_____
_____
_____

Water Intake

🥛 🥛 🥛 🥛 🥛 🥛 🥛 🥛 🥛

Hunger Scale

1   2   3   4   5   6   7   8   9   10

starving   So Full

I Ate Because

☐ STARVING   ☐ CRAVINGS   ☐ TROUBLED   ☐ MOODY   ☐ NEED FUEL

Symptoms/Feelings Post Meal ⟶ How Long After Meal?

☐ STRONG   ☐ BLOATING   ☐ DIGESTIVE   ☐ < 1HOUR   ☐ 1 - 2 HOURS

☐ FOCUSED   ☐ FOGGY MIND   ☐ OTHER _____

what? where? When? Why?

How do I feel when I enforce a healthy diet? _____

_____
_____
_____
_____
_____

Date: _____ Sleep Time: _____ 😁 🙂 😐 🙁 😫

☕ Breakfast   🌮 Lunch   🍃 Dinner

_____   _____   _____
_____   _____   _____
_____   _____   _____
_____   _____   _____
_____   _____   _____

🧁 Snack   ___ Water Intake ___

_____   ⌷ ⌷ ⌷ ⌷ ⌷ ⌷ ⌷ ⌷ ⌷
_____
_____   ___ Hunger Scale ___
_____
                        1 2 3 4 5 6 7 8 9 10
                        starving   So Full

___ I Ate Because ___

☐ STARVING ☐ CRAVINGS ☐ TROUBLED ☐ MOODY ☐ NEED FUEL

Symptoms/Feelings Post Meal ➔ How Long After Meal?

☐ STRONG   ☐ BLOATING   ☐ DIGESTIVE   ☐ < 1HOUR   ☐ 1 - 2 HOURS
☐ FOCUSED   ☐ FOGGY MIND ☐ OTHER _____

what? where? When? Why?

What are three things I can do regularly to reduce stress? _____

_____
_____
_____
_____

Date: _____ Sleep Time: _____ 😁 🙂 😐 🙁 😣

☕ Breakfast   🌮 Lunch   🍲 Dinner

_____   _____   _____
_____   _____   _____
_____   _____   _____
_____   _____   _____
_____   _____   _____

🧁 Snack

_____

_____

_____

_____

Water Intake

[glass] [glass] [glass] [glass] [glass] [glass] [glass] [glass] [glass]

Hunger Scale

1   2   3   4   5   6   7   8   9   10

starving   So Full

I Ate Because

☐ STARVING   ☐ CRAVINGS   ☐ TROUBLED   ☐ MOODY   ☐ NEED FUEL

Symptoms/Feelings Post Meal ⟶ How Long After Meal?

☐ STRONG   ☐ BLOATING   ☐ DIGESTIVE   ☐ < 1HOUR   ☐ 1 - 2 HOURS

☐ FOCUSED   ☐ FOGGY MIND   ☐ OTHER _____

what? where? When? Why?

What actions can I take to get closer to, or acquire the things
I need to grow? _____

_____

_____

_____

_____

Date: _____ Sleep Time: _____ 😁 🙂 😐 🙁 😣

☕ Breakfast   🌮 Lunch   🍜 Dinner

_____   _____   _____
_____   _____   _____
_____   _____   _____
_____   _____   _____
_____   _____   _____

🧁 Snack

_____   ——————— Water Intake ———————
_____   [ ] [ ] [ ] [ ] [ ] [ ] [ ] [ ] [ ]
_____
_____   ——————— Hunger Scale ———————
_____   1 2 3 4 5 6 7 8 9 10
_____ |————————————————————|
                           starving   So Full

——————— I Ate Because ———————
☐ STARVING   ☐ CRAVINGS   ☐ TROUBLED   ☐ MOODY   ☐ NEED FUEL

— Symptoms/Feelings Post Meal ——→ How Long After Meal? —
☐ STRONG   ☐ BLOATING   ☐ DIGESTIVE   ☐ < 1HOUR   ☐ 1 - 2 HOURS
☐ FOCUSED   ☐ FOGGY MIND   ☐ OTHER _____

what? where? When? Why?

What are the things I want to pay closer attention to this year? ———

_____
_____
_____
_____

Date:_____ Sleep Time: _____ 😄 🙂 😐 ☹️ 😣

☕ Breakfast   🌮 Lunch   🍜 Dinner

_____   _____   _____
_____   _____   _____
_____   _____   _____
_____   _____   _____
_____   _____   _____

🧁 Snack

_____

_____ Water Intake _____
[ ] [ ] [ ] [ ] [ ] [ ] [ ] [ ] [ ]

_____

_____ Hunger Scale _____
1 2 3 4 5 6 7 8 9 10
|—————————————————————————|
starving   So Full

_____

_____

_____ I Ate Because _____
☐ STARVING   ☐ CRAVINGS   ☐ TROUBLED   ☐ MOODY   ☐ NEED FUEL

— Symptoms/Feelings Post Meal ——→ How Long After Meal? —
☐ STRONG   ☐ BLOATING   ☐ DIGESTIVE   ☐ < 1HOUR   ☐ 1 - 2 HOURS
☐ FOCUSED   ☐ FOGGY MIND   ☐ OTHER

what? where? When? Why?

Do I feel and express enough gratitude and appreciation for what I have?

_____
_____
_____
_____
_____

Date: _____ Sleep Time: _____ 😄 🙂 😐 🙁 😣

☕ Breakfast   🌮 Lunch   🍝 Dinner

_____   _____   _____
_____   _____   _____
_____   _____   _____
_____   _____   _____
_____   _____   _____

🧁 Snack

_____

_____   _____ Water Intake _____

_____   [ ] [ ] [ ] [ ] [ ] [ ] [ ] [ ] [ ]

_____   _____ Hunger Scale _____

                          1   2   3   4   5   6   7   8   9   10
                          |----------------------------------|
                          starving   So Full

_____ I Ate Because _____

☐ STARVING   ☐ CRAVINGS   ☐ TROUBLED   ☐ MOODY   ☐ NEED FUEL

─ Symptoms/Feelings Post Meal ──────▶ How Long After Meal? ─

☐ STRONG   ☐ BLOATING   ☐ DIGESTIVE   ☐ < 1HOUR   ☐ 1 - 2 HOURS

☐ FOCUSED   ☐ FOGGY MIND ☐ OTHER _____

what? where? When? Why?

What enjoyable activity do I not engage in often enough? _____

_____
_____
_____
_____

Date: _____ Sleep Time: _____ 😄 🙂 😐 🙁 😫

☕ Breakfast   🌮 Lunch   🍳 Dinner

_____   _____   _____

_____   _____   _____

_____   _____   _____

_____   _____   _____

_____   _____   _____

🧁 Snack

_____

_____

_____

_____

Water Intake

🥛 🥛 🥛 🥛 🥛 🥛 🥛 🥛 🥛

Hunger Scale

1   2   3   4   5   6   7   8   9   10

starving   So Full

I Ate Because

☐ STARVING   ☐ CRAVINGS   ☐ TROUBLED   ☐ MOODY   ☐ NEED FUEL

Symptoms/Feelings Post Meal ➡ How Long After Meal?

☐ STRONG   ☐ BLOATING   ☐ DIGESTIVE   ☐ < 1HOUR   ☐ 1 - 2 HOURS

☐ FOCUSED   ☐ FOGGY MIND   ☐ OTHER _____

what? where? When? Why?

How do I feel when I have extremely uncomfortably full? _____

_____

_____

_____

_____

_____

Date: _____ Sleep Time: _____ 😄 🙂 😐 🙁 😣

☕ Breakfast

_____
_____
_____
_____
_____

🌮 Lunch

_____
_____
_____
_____
_____

🍽 Dinner

_____
_____
_____
_____
_____

🧁 Snack

_____
_____
_____
_____

Water Intake _____

🥛 🥛 🥛 🥛 🥛 🥛 🥛 🥛 🥛

Hunger Scale _____

1   2   3   4   5   6   7   8   9   10

starving   So Full

I Ate Because

☐ STARVING   ☐ CRAVINGS   ☐ TROUBLED   ☐ MOODY   ☐ NEED FUEL

Symptoms/Feelings Post Meal ⟶ How Long After Meal?

☐ STRONG   ☐ BLOATING   ☐ DIGESTIVE   ☐ < 1HOUR   ☐ 1 - 2 HOURS

☐ FOCUSED   ☐ FOGGY MIND   ☐ OTHER _____

what? where? When? Why?

Am I holding onto (food) that would be better to let go of ? _____

_____
_____
_____
_____

Date: _____ Sleep Time: _____ 😄 🙂 😐 🙁 😣

☕ Breakfast   🌮 Lunch   🍜 Dinner

_____   _____   _____
_____   _____   _____
_____   _____   _____
_____   _____   _____
_____   _____   _____

🧁 Snack

_____

_____

_____

_____

Water Intake

[glass] [glass] [glass] [glass] [glass] [glass] [glass] [glass] [glass]

Hunger Scale

1   2   3   4   5   6   7   8   9   10

starving   So Full

I Ate Because

☐ STARVING   ☐ CRAVINGS   ☐ TROUBLED   ☐ MOODY   ☐ NEED FUEL

Symptoms/Feelings Post Meal ⟶ How Long After Meal?

☐ STRONG   ☐ BLOATING   ☐ DIGESTIVE   ☐ < 1HOUR   ☐ 1 - 2 HOURS

☐ FOCUSED   ☐ FOGGY MIND   ☐ OTHER _____

what? where? When? Why?

I feel lively when _____

_____

_____

_____

_____

Date: _____ Sleep Time: _____ 😁 🙂 😐 🙁 😣

☕ Breakfast

_____
_____
_____
_____

🌮 Lunch

_____
_____
_____
_____

🍽 Dinner

_____
_____
_____
_____

🧁 Snack

_____
_____
_____

Water Intake

[ ] [ ] [ ] [ ] [ ] [ ] [ ] [ ] [ ]

Hunger Scale

1   2   3   4   5   6   7   8   9   10

starving   So Full

I Ate Because

[ ] STARVING   [ ] CRAVINGS   [ ] TROUBLED   [ ] MOODY   [ ] NEED FUEL

Symptoms/Feelings Post Meal ———➤ How Long After Meal?

[ ] STRONG   [ ] BLOATING   [ ] DIGESTIVE   [ ] < 1HOUR   [ ] 1 - 2 HOURS

[ ] FOCUSED   [ ] FOGGY MIND   [ ] OTHER _____

what? where? When? Why?

Do I have enough support from friends and family to help me achieve
the personal growth I desire? _____

_____
_____
_____

Date: _____   Sleep Time: _____   😁 ☺ 😐 🙁 😣

☕ Breakfast   🌮 Lunch   🍃 Dinner
_____   _____   _____
_____   _____   _____
_____   _____   _____
_____   _____   _____

🧁 Snack

_____

_____

_____

_____

Water Intake

[🥛 🥛 🥛 🥛 🥛 🥛 🥛 🥛 🥛]

Hunger Scale

1   2   3   4   5   6   7   8   9   10
starving   So Full

I Ate Because

☐ STARVING   ☐ CRAVINGS   ☐ TROUBLED   ☐ MOODY   ☐ NEED FUEL

Symptoms/Feelings Post Meal ⟶ How Long After Meal?

☐ STRONG   ☐ BLOATING   ☐ DIGESTIVE   ☐ < 1HOUR   ☐ 1 - 2 HOURS

☐ FOCUSED   ☐ FOGGY MIND   ☐ OTHER _____

what? where? When? Why?

What am I most proud of ? _____
_____
_____
_____
_____
_____

Date: _____ Sleep Time: _____ 😁 🙂 😐 🙁 😣

☕ Breakfast
_____
_____
_____
_____
_____

🌮 Lunch
_____
_____
_____
_____
_____

🍝 Dinner
_____
_____
_____
_____
_____

🧁 Snack
_____
_____
_____
_____

Water Intake

[ ] [ ] [ ] [ ] [ ] [ ] [ ] [ ] [ ]

Hunger Scale

1 2 3 4 5 6 7 8 9 10

starving   So Full

I Ate Because

[ ] STARVING [ ] CRAVINGS [ ] TROUBLED [ ] MOODY [ ] NEED FUEL

Symptoms/Feelings Post Meal ⟶ How Long After Meal?

[ ] STRONG   [ ] BLOATING   [ ] DIGESTIVE   [ ] < 1HOUR   [ ] 1 - 2 HOURS

[ ] FOCUSED [ ] FOGGY MIND [ ] OTHER _____

what? where? When? Why?

Do I give myself enough credit? _____
_____
_____
_____
_____
_____

Date: _____ Sleep Time: _____ 😁 🙂 😐 ☹️ 😣

☕ Breakfast
_____
_____
_____
_____
_____

🌮 Lunch
_____
_____
_____
_____
_____

🍝 Dinner
_____
_____
_____
_____
_____

🧁 Snack
_____
_____
_____
_____

Water Intake

Hunger Scale

1	2	3	4	5	6	7	8	9	10

starving   So Full

I Ate Because

☐ STARVING   ☐ CRAVINGS   ☐ TROUBLED   ☐ MOODY   ☐ NEED FUEL

Symptoms/Feelings Post Meal ➞ How Long After Meal?

☐ STRONG   ☐ BLOATING   ☐ DIGESTIVE   ☐ < 1HOUR   ☐ 1 - 2 HOURS

☐ FOCUSED   ☐ FOGGY MIND   ☐ OTHER _____

what? where? When? Why?

What steps can I take to eliminate anxiety (about food)? _____
_____
_____
_____
_____
_____

Date: _____ Sleep Time: _____ 😄 🙂 😐 🙁 😣

☕ Breakfast   🌮 Lunch   🍝 Dinner

_____   _____   _____

_____   _____   _____

_____   _____   _____

_____   _____   _____

🧁 Snack

_____

Water Intake

🥛 🥛 🥛 🥛 🥛 🥛 🥛 🥛 🥛

_____

Hunger Scale

| 1 | 2 | 3 | 4 | 5 | 6 | 7 | 8 | 9 | 10 |

starving   So Full

_____

I Ate Because

☐ STARVING   ☐ CRAVINGS   ☐ TROUBLED   ☐ MOODY   ☐ NEED FUEL

Symptoms/Feelings Post Meal ⟶ How Long After Meal?

☐ STRONG   ☐ BLOATING   ☐ DIGESTIVE   ☐ < 1HOUR   ☐ 1 - 2 HOURS

☐ FOCUSED   ☐ FOGGY MIND   ☐ OTHER _____

what? where? When? Why?

Have I had a negative food diet experience? _____

_____

_____

_____

Date: _____ Sleep Time: _____ 😄 🙂 😐 🙁 😣

☕ Breakfast 🌮 Lunch 🍝 Dinner

_____ _____ _____
_____ _____ _____
_____ _____ _____
_____ _____ _____
_____ _____ _____

🧁 Snack

_____

_____

_____

_____

Water Intake

🥛 🥛 🥛 🥛 🥛 🥛 🥛 🥛 🥛

Hunger Scale

1 2 3 4 5 6 7 8 9 10

starving   So Full

I Ate Because

☐ STARVING ☐ CRAVINGS ☐ TROUBLED ☐ MOODY ☐ NEED FUEL

Symptoms/Feelings Post Meal ➞ How Long After Meal?

☐ STRONG ☐ BLOATING ☐ DIGESTIVE ☐ < 1HOUR ☐ 1 - 2 HOURS

☐ FOCUSED ☐ FOGGY MIND ☐ OTHER _____

what? where? When? Why?

What is my last mistake and what did you learn from it? _____

_____

_____

_____

_____

_____

Date: _____ Sleep Time: _____ 😄 🙂 😐 ☹️ 😣

☕ Breakfast   🌮 Lunch   🍽 Dinner

_____   _____   _____
_____   _____   _____
_____   _____   _____
_____   _____   _____

🧁 Snack

_____

_____

_____

_____

____ Water Intake ____

[glass] [glass] [glass] [glass] [glass] [glass] [glass] [glass] [glass]

____ Hunger Scale ____

1   2   3   4   5   6   7   8   9   10
├──────────────────────────────────┤
starving   So Full

_____ I Ate Because _____

☐ STARVING   ☐ CRAVINGS   ☐ TROUBLED   ☐ MOODY   ☐ NEED FUEL

__ Symptoms/Feelings Post Meal ──→ How Long After Meal? __

☐ STRONG   ☐ BLOATING   ☐ DIGESTIVE   ☐ < 1HOUR   ☐ 1 - 2 HOURS

☐ FOCUSED   ☐ FOGGY MIND   ☐ OTHER _____

what? where? When? Why?

When I feel emotional pain, what are five things I can do for myself?

- _____
- _____
- _____
- _____
- _____

Date: _____ Sleep Time: _____ 😄 🙂 😐 🙁 😣

☕ Breakfast   🌮 Lunch   🥗 Dinner

_____   _____   _____
_____   _____   _____
_____   _____   _____
_____   _____   _____
_____   _____   _____

🧁 Snack

_____

_____

_____

_____

Water Intake

[ ] [ ] [ ] [ ] [ ] [ ] [ ] [ ] [ ]

Hunger Scale

1   2   3   4   5   6   7   8   9   10

starving   So Full

I Ate Because

[ ] STARVING   [ ] CRAVINGS   [ ] TROUBLED   [ ] MOODY   [ ] NEED FUEL

Symptoms/Feelings Post Meal ⟶ How Long After Meal?

[ ] STRONG   [ ] BLOATING   [ ] DIGESTIVE   [ ] < 1HOUR   [ ] 1 - 2 HOURS

[ ] FOCUSED   [ ] FOGGY MIND   [ ] OTHER _____

what? where? When? Why?

If I can talk to myself a year ago, the only thing I want to say is _____

_____

_____

_____

_____

_____

Date: _____ Sleep Time: _____ 😄 🙂 😐 🙁 😣

☕ Breakfast

_____
_____
_____
_____
_____

🌮 Lunch

_____
_____
_____
_____
_____

🍳 Dinner

_____
_____
_____
_____
_____

🧁 Snack

_____
_____
_____
_____

Water Intake

🥛 🥛 🥛 🥛 🥛 🥛 🥛 🥛 🥛

Hunger Scale

1	2	3	4	5	6	7	8	9	10

starving   So Full

I Ate Because

☐ STARVING ☐ CRAVINGS ☐ TROUBLED ☐ MOODY ☐ NEED FUEL

Symptoms/Feelings Post Meal ➙ How Long After Meal?

☐ STRONG   ☐ BLOATING   ☐ DIGESTIVE   ☐ < 1HOUR   ☐ 1 - 2 HOURS

☐ FOCUSED   ☐ FOGGY MIND   ☐ OTHER _____

what? where? When? Why?

What are my five major strengths? _____

_____
_____
_____
_____
_____

Date: _____ Sleep Time: _____ 😄 🙂 😐 🙁 😣

☕ Breakfast   🌮 Lunch   🍲 Dinner

_____   _____   _____
_____   _____   _____
_____   _____   _____
_____   _____   _____
_____   _____   _____

🧁 Snack

_____
_____
_____
_____

Water Intake

[glass] [glass] [glass] [glass] [glass] [glass] [glass] [glass] [glass]

Hunger Scale

1   2   3   4   5   6   7   8   9   10

starving   So Full

I Ate Because

☐ STARVING   ☐ CRAVINGS   ☐ TROUBLED   ☐ MOODY   ☐ NEED FUEL

Symptoms/Feelings Post Meal ➔ How Long After Meal?

☐ STRONG   ☐ BLOATING   ☐ DIGESTIVE   ☐ < 1HOUR   ☐ 1 - 2 HOURS

☐ FOCUSED   ☐ FOGGY MIND   ☐ OTHER _____

what? where? When? Why?

Today while eating (dinner), Am I busy or calm? _____

_____
_____
_____
_____
_____

Date: _____ Sleep Time: _____ 😄 ☺ 😐 ☹ 😣

☕ Breakfast

_____
_____
_____
_____
_____

🌮 Lunch

_____
_____
_____
_____
_____

🍝 Dinner

_____
_____
_____
_____
_____

🧁 Snack

_____
_____
_____
_____

Water Intake

🥛 🥛 🥛 🥛 🥛 🥛 🥛 🥛 🥛

Hunger Scale

1 2 3 4 5 6 7 8 9 10

starving   So Full

I Ate Because

☐ STARVING ☐ CRAVINGS ☐ TROUBLED ☐ MOODY ☐ NEED FUEL

Symptoms/Feelings Post Meal ➡ How Long After Meal?

☐ STRONG ☐ BLOATING ☐ DIGESTIVE ☐ < 1HOUR ☐ 1 - 2 HOURS

☐ FOCUSED ☐ FOGGY MIND ☐ OTHER _____

what? where? When? Why?

I feel stress when _____
_____
_____
_____
_____
_____

Date: _____ Sleep Time: _____ 😁 ☺ 😐 ☹ 😣

☕ Breakfast   🌮 Lunch   🍝 Dinner

_____   _____   _____
_____   _____   _____
_____   _____   _____
_____   _____   _____
_____   _____   _____

🧁 Snack

_____

_____

_____

_____

Water Intake

[ ] [ ] [ ] [ ] [ ] [ ] [ ] [ ] [ ]

Hunger Scale

1   2   3   4   5   6   7   8   9   10

starving   So Full

I Ate Because

[ ] STARVING   [ ] CRAVINGS   [ ] TROUBLED   [ ] MOODY   [ ] NEED FUEL

Symptoms/Feelings Post Meal ⟶ How Long After Meal?

[ ] STRONG   [ ] BLOATING   [ ] DIGESTIVE   [ ] < 1HOUR   [ ] 1 - 2 HOURS

[ ] FOCUSED   [ ] FOGGY MIND   [ ] OTHER _____

what? where? When? Why?

Do I easily feel frustrated or angry when I am not achieving my goals?

_____

_____

_____

_____

_____

Date: _____ Sleep Time: _____ 😄 🙂 😐 🙁 😣

☕ Breakfast   🌮 Lunch   🍝 Dinner

_____   _____   _____
_____   _____   _____
_____   _____   _____
_____   _____   _____
_____   _____   _____

🧁 Snack

_____

_____   _____ Water Intake _____

_____   [🥤] [🥤] [🥤] [🥤] [🥤] [🥤] [🥤] [🥤] [🥤]

_____   _____ Hunger Scale _____

                          1   2   3   4   5   6   7   8   9   10
                          starving   So Full

_____ I Ate Because _____

☐ STARVING   ☐ CRAVINGS   ☐ TROUBLED   ☐ MOODY   ☐ NEED FUEL

Symptoms/Feelings Post Meal ──────▶ How Long After Meal?

☐ STRONG   ☐ BLOATING   ☐ DIGESTIVE   ☐ < 1HOUR   ☐ 1 - 2 HOURS

☐ FOCUSED   ☐ FOGGY MIND ☐ OTHER _____

what? where? When? Why?

Deep inside, do I know that there is more than one way to achieve
a better outcome? _____

_____

_____

_____

Date: _____ Sleep Time: _____ 😄 🙂 😐 🙁 😣

☕ Breakfast   🌮 Lunch   🍝 Dinner

_____   _____   _____
_____   _____   _____
_____   _____   _____
_____   _____   _____
_____   _____   _____

🧁 Snack

_____
_____
_____
_____

Water Intake

🥛 🥛 🥛 🥛 🥛 🥛 🥛 🥛 🥛

Hunger Scale

1   2   3   4   5   6   7   8   9   10
starving   So Full

I Ate Because

☐ STARVING   ☐ CRAVINGS   ☐ TROUBLED   ☐ MOODY   ☐ NEED FUEL

Symptoms/Feelings Post Meal ➡ **How Long After Meal?**

☐ STRONG   ☐ BLOATING   ☐ DIGESTIVE   ☐ < 1HOUR   ☐ 1 - 2 HOURS
☐ FOCUSED   ☐ FOGGY MIND ☐ OTHER _____

what? where? When? Why?

What are things that really important to me? _____

_____
_____
_____
_____
_____

Date: _____ Sleep Time: _____ 😄 🙂 😐 🙁 😣

☕ Breakfast   🌮 Lunch   🍽 Dinner

_____   _____   _____
_____   _____   _____
_____   _____   _____
_____   _____   _____
_____   _____   _____

🧁 Snack

_____

——— Water Intake ———

🥛 🥛 🥛 🥛 🥛 🥛 🥛 🥛 🥛

_____

——— Hunger Scale ———

1 2 3 4 5 6 7 8 9 10

starving   So Full

——— I Ate Because ———

☐ STARVING ☐ CRAVINGS ☐ TROUBLED ☐ MOODY ☐ NEED FUEL

Symptoms/Feelings Post Meal ——→ How Long After Meal?

☐ STRONG   ☐ BLOATING   ☐ DIGESTIVE   ☐ < 1HOUR   ☐ 1 - 2 HOURS

☐ FOCUSED ☐ FOGGY MIND ☐ OTHER _____

what? where? When? Why?

What are the things I am proud of in my life so far? _____

_____
_____
_____
_____
_____

Date:_____ Sleep Time: _____ 😁 🙂 😐 🙁 😣

☕ Breakfast ⋯⋯⋯⋯⋯ 🌮 Lunch ⋯⋯⋯⋯⋯ 🍃 Dinner

_____ _____ _____
_____ _____ _____
_____ _____ _____
_____ _____ _____
_____ _____ _____

🧁 Snack

_____
_____
_____
_____
_____

Water Intake

[glass] [glass] [glass] [glass] [glass] [glass] [glass] [glass] [glass]

Hunger Scale

1 2 3 4 5 6 7 8 9 10

starving   So Full

I Ate Because

☐ STARVING ☐ CRAVINGS ☐ TROUBLED ☐ MOODY ☐ NEED FUEL

Symptoms/Feelings Post Meal ⟶ How Long After Meal?

☐ STRONG ☐ BLOATING ☐ DIGESTIVE ☐ < 1HOUR ☐ 1 - 2 HOURS

☐ FOCUSED ☐ FOGGY MIND ☐ OTHER _____

what? where? When? Why?

Which of my talents or skills gives me the greatest sense of pride
or satisfaction? _____

_____
_____
_____
_____

Date: _____ Sleep Time: _____ 😄 🙂 😐 🙁 😫

☕ Breakfast　　　🌮 Lunch　　　🍳 Dinner

_____　　　_____　　　_____
_____　　　_____　　　_____
_____　　　_____　　　_____
_____　　　_____　　　_____

🧁 Snack

_____

_____

_____

_____

Water Intake

🥛 🥛 🥛 🥛 🥛 🥛 🥛 🥛 🥛

Hunger Scale

1　2　3　4　5　6　7　8　9　10

starving　　　　　　　　　　So Full

I Ate Because

☐ STARVING　☐ CRAVINGS　☐ TROUBLED　☐ MOODY　☐ NEED FUEL

Symptoms/Feelings Post Meal ➤ How Long After Meal?

☐ STRONG　☐ BLOATING　☐ DIGESTIVE　☐ < 1HOUR　☐ 1 - 2 HOURS

☐ FOCUSED　☐ FOGGY MIND　☐ OTHER

what? where? When? Why?

I feel happier in my skin when _____

_____

_____

_____

_____

Date: _____   Sleep Time: _____   😄 🙂 😐 🙁 😣

☕ Breakfast   🌮 Lunch   🍝 Dinner
_____   _____   _____
_____   _____   _____
_____   _____   _____
_____   _____   _____

🧁 Snack

_____

_____   Water Intake
                    🥛 🥛 🥛 🥛 🥛 🥛 🥛 🥛 🥛
_____

_____   Hunger Scale

                    1   2   3   4   5   6   7   8   9   10
                    ├─────────────────────────────────────┤
                    starving   So Full

─────── I Ate Because ───────
☐ STARVING   ☐ CRAVINGS   ☐ TROUBLED   ☐ MOODY   ☐ NEED FUEL

── Symptoms/Feelings Post Meal ──➤ How Long After Meal? ──
☐ STRONG   ☐ BLOATING   ☐ DIGESTIVE   ☐ < 1HOUR   ☐ 1 - 2 HOURS
☐ FOCUSED   ☐ FOGGY MIND ☐ OTHER _____

what? where? When? Why?

My favorite way to spend the day is _____
_____
_____
_____
_____
_____

Date: _____ Sleep Time: _____ 😄 🙂 😐 🙁 😣

☕ Breakfast   🌮 Lunch   🍳 Dinner

_____   _____   _____
_____   _____   _____
_____   _____   _____
_____   _____   _____
_____   _____   _____

🧁 Snack

_____

_____

_____

_____

_____ Water Intake _____

| 🥛 | 🥛 | 🥛 | 🥛 | 🥛 | 🥛 | 🥛 | 🥛 | 🥛 |

_____ Hunger Scale _____

1   2   3   4   5   6   7   8   9   10

starving   So Full

_____ I Ate Because _____

☐ STARVING   ☐ CRAVINGS   ☐ TROUBLED   ☐ MOODY   ☐ NEED FUEL

__ Symptoms/Feelings Post Meal ⟶ How Long After Meal? __

☐ STRONG   ☐ BLOATING   ☐ DIGESTIVE   ☐ < 1HOUR   ☐ 1 - 2 HOURS

☐ FOCUSED   ☐ FOGGY MIND ☐ OTHER _____

what? where? When? Why?

How much do I trust myself? _____

_____
_____
_____
_____
_____

Date: _____ Sleep Time: _____ 😁 🙂 😐 ☹️ 😣

☕ Breakfast   🌮 Lunch   🍃 Dinner

_____   _____   _____
_____   _____   _____
_____   _____   _____
_____   _____   _____
_____   _____   _____

🧁 Snack

_____

_____   _____ Water Intake _____

_____ | 🥛 🥛 🥛 🥛 🥛 🥛 🥛 🥛 🥛 |

_____   _____ Hunger Scale _____

_____ | 1 2 3 4 5 6 7 8 9 10 |
                       | starving   So Full |

_____ I Ate Because _____

☐ STARVING   ☐ CRAVINGS   ☐ TROUBLED   ☐ MOODY   ☐ NEED FUEL

┌ Symptoms/Feelings Post Meal ───▶ How Long After Meal? ┐

☐ STRONG   ☐ BLOATING   ☐ DIGESTIVE   ☐ < 1HOUR   ☐ 1 - 2 HOURS

☐ FOCUSED   ☐ FOGGY MIND   ☐ OTHER _____

what? where? When? Why?

What are some tough questions about my health? _____

_____
_____
_____
_____
_____

Date: _____ Sleep Time: _____ 😄 🙂 😐 ☹️ 😣

☕ Breakfast   🌮 Lunch   🍃 Dinner

_____   _____   _____
_____   _____   _____
_____   _____   _____
_____   _____   _____
_____   _____   _____

🧁 Snack

_____

_____ Water Intake _____

🥛 🥛 🥛 🥛 🥛 🥛 🥛 🥛 🥛

_____

_____ Hunger Scale _____

1 2 3 4 5 6 7 8 9 10

starving   So Full

_____

_____ I Ate Because _____

☐ STARVING   ☐ CRAVINGS   ☐ TROUBLED   ☐ MOODY   ☐ NEED FUEL

Symptoms/Feelings Post Meal ➡️ How Long After Meal?

☐ STRONG   ☐ BLOATING   ☐ DIGESTIVE   ☐ < 1HOUR   ☐ 1 - 2 HOURS

☐ FOCUSED   ☐ FOGGY MIND   ☐ OTHER _____

what? where? When? Why?

Am I willing to ask for the support I need? _____

_____
_____
_____
_____

Date: _____ Sleep Time: _____ 😄 🙂 😐 🙁 😣

☕ Breakfast   🌮 Lunch   🍳 Dinner

_____   _____   _____
_____   _____   _____
_____   _____   _____
_____   _____   _____

🧁 Snack

_____

_____

_____

_____

Water Intake

[ ] [ ] [ ] [ ] [ ] [ ] [ ] [ ] [ ]

Hunger Scale

1   2   3   4   5   6   7   8   9   10

starving   So Full

I Ate Because

☐ STARVING   ☐ CRAVINGS   ☐ TROUBLED   ☐ MOODY   ☐ NEED FUEL

Symptoms/Feelings Post Meal ⟶ How Long After Meal?

☐ STRONG   ☐ BLOATING   ☐ DIGESTIVE   ☐ < 1HOUR   ☐ 1 - 2 HOURS

☐ FOCUSED   ☐ FOGGY MIND   ☐ OTHER _____

what? where? When? Why?

What are my greatest talents or skills? _____

_____

_____

_____

_____

_____

Date: _____ Sleep Time: _____ 😄 🙂 😐 🙁 😣

☕ Breakfast   🌮 Lunch   🍵 Dinner

_____   _____   _____
_____   _____   _____
_____   _____   _____
_____   _____   _____
_____   _____   _____

🧁 Snack

_____

_____ Water Intake _____

| 🥛 | 🥛 | 🥛 | 🥛 | 🥛 | 🥛 | 🥛 | 🥛 | 🥛 |

_____

_____   _____ Hunger Scale _____

_____   1   2   3   4   5   6   7   8   9   10
_____   starving   So Full

_____ I Ate Because _____

☐ STARVING   ☐ CRAVINGS   ☐ TROUBLED   ☐ MOODY   ☐ NEED FUEL

⌐ Symptoms/Feelings Post Meal ——→ How Long After Meal? ¬

☐ STRONG   ☐ BLOATING   ☐ DIGESTIVE   ☐ < 1HOUR   ☐ 1 - 2 HOURS

☐ FOCUSED   ☐ FOGGY MIND ☐ OTHER

what? where? When? Why?

What would I like to stop worrying about? _____

_____
_____
_____
_____
_____

Date:_____ Sleep Time: _____ 😄 🙂 😐 🙁 😣

☕ Breakfast   🌮 Lunch   🍃 Dinner

_____   _____   _____
_____   _____   _____
_____   _____   _____
_____   _____   _____
_____   _____   _____

🧁 Snack

_____

_____   ___ Water Intake ___

_____   [🥛 🥛 🥛 🥛 🥛 🥛 🥛 🥛 🥛]

_____   ___ Hunger Scale ___

                    1 2 3 4 5 6 7 8 9 10
                    ├─
                    starving   So Full

─────────────── I Ate Because ───────────────
☐ STARVING   ☐ CRAVINGS   ☐ TROUBLED   ☐ MOODY   ☐ NEED FUEL

─ Symptoms/Feelings Post Meal ──→ How Long After Meal? ─
☐ STRONG   ☐ BLOATING   ☐ DIGESTIVE   ☐ < 1HOUR   ☐ 1 - 2 HOURS
☐ FOCUSED   ☐ FOGGY MIND ☐ OTHER _____

what? where? When? Why?

What's one thing I would like to do more of and why? How can I make
that happen? _____

_____

_____

_____

Date: _____ Sleep Time: _____ 😄 🙂 😐 ☹️ 😣

☕ Breakfast
_____
_____
_____
_____
_____

🌮 Lunch
_____
_____
_____
_____
_____

🍽️ Dinner
_____
_____
_____
_____
_____

🧁 Snack
_____
_____
_____
_____

Water Intake
🥛 🥛 🥛 🥛 🥛 🥛 🥛 🥛 🥛

Hunger Scale
1 2 3 4 5 6 7 8 9 10
starving   So Full

I Ate Because
☐ STARVING ☐ CRAVINGS ☐ TROUBLED ☐ MOODY ☐ NEED FUEL

Symptoms/Feelings Post Meal → How Long After Meal?
☐ STRONG ☐ BLOATING ☐ DIGESTIVE ☐ < 1HOUR ☐ 1 - 2 HOURS
☐ FOCUSED ☐ FOGGY MIND ☐ OTHER _____

what? where? When? Why?

Which five words describe me best? _____
_____
_____
_____
_____
_____

Date: _____ Sleep Time: _____ 😄 🙂 😐 🙁 😣

☕ Breakfast

_____
_____
_____
_____
_____

🌮 Lunch

_____
_____
_____
_____
_____

🍝 Dinner

_____
_____
_____
_____
_____

🧁 Snack

_____
_____
_____
_____

Water Intake

🥛 🥛 🥛 🥛 🥛 🥛 🥛 🥛 🥛

Hunger Scale

1   2   3   4   5   6   7   8   9   10

starving   So Full

I Ate Because

☐ STARVING   ☐ CRAVINGS   ☐ TROUBLED   ☐ MOODY   ☐ NEED FUEL

Symptoms/Feelings Post Meal ⟶ How Long After Meal?

☐ STRONG   ☐ BLOATING   ☐ DIGESTIVE   ☐ < 1HOUR   ☐ 1 - 2 HOURS

☐ FOCUSED   ☐ FOGGY MIND   ☐ OTHER _____

what? where? When? Why?

What are my most important needs and desires? _____

_____
_____
_____
_____
_____

Date: _____ Sleep Time: _____ 😄 🙂 😐 🙁 😣

☕ Breakfast

_____
_____
_____
_____
_____

🌮 Lunch

_____
_____
_____
_____
_____

🍲 Dinner

_____
_____
_____
_____
_____

🧁 Snack

_____
_____
_____
_____

Water Intake

🥛 🥛 🥛 🥛 🥛 🥛 🥛 🥛 🥛

Hunger Scale

1   2   3   4   5   6   7   8   9   10
starving   So Full

I Ate Because

☐ STARVING   ☐ CRAVINGS   ☐ TROUBLED   ☐ MOODY   ☐ NEED FUEL

Symptoms/Feelings Post Meal ➔ How Long After Meal?

☐ STRONG   ☐ BLOATING   ☐ DIGESTIVE   ☐ < 1HOUR   ☐ 1 - 2 HOURS

☐ FOCUSED   ☐ FOGGY MIND   ☐ OTHER _____

what? where? When? Why?

What are my personal gifts? _____
_____
_____
_____
_____
_____

Date: _____ Sleep Time: _____ 😄 🙂 😐 🙁 😣

☕ Breakfast   🌮 Lunch   🍝 Dinner
_____   _____   _____
_____   _____   _____
_____   _____   _____
_____   _____   _____
_____   _____   _____

🧁 Snack   _____ Water Intake _____
_____   [🥛] [🥛] [🥛] [🥛] [🥛] [🥛] [🥛] [🥛] [🥛]
_____
_____   _____ Hunger Scale _____
_____   1   2   3   4   5   6   7   8   9   10
_____   starving   So Full

_____ I Ate Because _____
☐ STARVING   ☐ CRAVINGS   ☐ TROUBLED   ☐ MOODY   ☐ NEED FUEL

__ Symptoms/Feelings Post Meal __ ➔ How Long After Meal? __
☐ STRONG   ☐ BLOATING   ☐ DIGESTIVE   ☐ < 1HOUR   ☐ 1 - 2 HOURS
☐ FOCUSED   ☐ FOGGY MIND ☐ OTHER _____

what? where? When? Why?

When do I think about eating? _____
_____
_____
_____
_____
_____

Date: _____ Sleep Time: _____ 😄 ☺ 😐 🙁 😣

☕ Breakfast   🌮 Lunch   🍝 Dinner

_____   _____   _____
_____   _____   _____
_____   _____   _____
_____   _____   _____
_____   _____   _____

🧁 Snack

_____

_____

_____

_____

_____

Water Intake

[glass] [glass] [glass] [glass] [glass] [glass] [glass] [glass] [glass]

Hunger Scale

1   2   3   4   5   6   7   8   9   10

starving   So Full

I Ate Because

☐ STARVING   ☐ CRAVINGS   ☐ TROUBLED   ☐ MOODY   ☐ NEED FUEL

Symptoms/Feelings Post Meal ⟶ How Long After Meal?

☐ STRONG   ☐ BLOATING   ☐ DIGESTIVE   ☐ < 1HOUR   ☐ 1 - 2 HOURS

☐ FOCUSED   ☐ FOGGY MIND   ☐ OTHER _____

what? where? When? Why?

When do I decide to eat? _____

_____

_____

_____

_____

Date: _____ Sleep Time: _____ 😄 🙂 😐 🙁 😣

☕ Breakfast   🌮 Lunch   🍝 Dinner

_____   _____   _____
_____   _____   _____
_____   _____   _____
_____   _____   _____
_____   _____   _____

🧁 Snack   Water Intake _____

_____   [glass][glass][glass][glass][glass][glass][glass][glass][glass]
_____
_____   Hunger Scale _____
_____
                    1 2 3 4 5 6 7 8 9 10
                    |————————————————————————|
                    starving   So Full

I Ate Because _____

☐ STARVING   ☐ CRAVINGS   ☐ TROUBLED   ☐ MOODY   ☐ NEED FUEL

Symptoms/Feelings Post Meal ——→ How Long After Meal?

☐ STRONG   ☐ BLOATING   ☐ DIGESTIVE   ☐ < 1HOUR   ☐ 1 - 2 HOURS

☐ FOCUSED   ☐ FOGGY MIND ☐ OTHER _____

what? where? When? Why?

What should I do to get more peace in my life? _____

_____

_____

_____

_____

Date: _____ Sleep Time: _____ 😄 🙂 😐 🙁 😫

☕ Breakfast

_____
_____
_____
_____
_____

🌮 Lunch

_____
_____
_____
_____
_____

🍳 Dinner

_____
_____
_____
_____
_____

🧁 Snack

_____
_____
_____
_____

Water Intake

[glass] [glass] [glass] [glass] [glass] [glass] [glass] [glass] [glass]

Hunger Scale

1 2 3 4 5 6 7 8 9 10

starving   So Full

I Ate Because

☐ STARVING   ☐ CRAVINGS   ☐ TROUBLED   ☐ MOODY   ☐ NEED FUEL

Symptoms/Feelings Post Meal ➡ How Long After Meal?

☐ STRONG   ☐ BLOATING   ☐ DIGESTIVE   ☐ < 1HOUR   ☐ 1 - 2 HOURS

☐ FOCUSED   ☐ FOGGY MIND ☐ OTHER _____

what? where? When? Why?

What do I "eat" choose from all the available options? _____

_____
_____
_____
_____
_____

Date: _____ Sleep Time: _____ 😄 🙂 😐 🙁 😖

☕ Breakfast   🌮 Lunch   🍝 Dinner

_____ _____ _____
_____ _____ _____
_____ _____ _____
_____ _____ _____
_____ _____ _____

🧁 Snack

_____

_____

_____

_____

Water Intake

[glass] [glass] [glass] [glass] [glass] [glass] [glass] [glass] [glass]

Hunger Scale

1   2   3   4   5   6   7   8   9   10

starving   So Full

I Ate Because

☐ STARVING   ☐ CRAVINGS   ☐ TROUBLED   ☐ MOODY   ☐ NEED FUEL

Symptoms/Feelings Post Meal ⟶ How Long After Meal?

☐ STRONG   ☐ BLOATING   ☐ DIGESTIVE   ☐ < 1HOUR   ☐ 1 - 2 HOURS

☐ FOCUSED   ☐ FOGGY MIND   ☐ OTHER _____

what? where? When? Why?

Where does the fuel I have consumed go? _____

_____

_____

_____

_____

_____

Date: _____ Sleep Time: _____ 😁 🙂 😐 🙁 😣

☕ Breakfast   🌮 Lunch   🍝 Dinner

_____   _____   _____
_____   _____   _____
_____   _____   _____
_____   _____   _____

🧁 Snack

_____
_____
_____
_____

Water Intake

Hunger Scale

1   2   3   4   5   6   7   8   9   10

starving   So Full

I Ate Because

☐ STARVING   ☐ CRAVINGS   ☐ TROUBLED   ☐ MOODY   ☐ NEED FUEL

Symptoms/Feelings Post Meal ⟶ How Long After Meal?

☐ STRONG   ☐ BLOATING   ☐ DIGESTIVE   ☐ < 1 HOUR   ☐ 1 - 2 HOURS

☐ FOCUSED   ☐ FOGGY MIND   ☐ OTHER _____

what? where? When? Why?

Am I living my passion? _____
_____
_____
_____
_____

Date: _____ Sleep Time: _____ 😄 🙂 😐 🙁 😣

☕ Breakfast   🌮 Lunch   🍜 Dinner

_____   _____   _____
_____   _____   _____
_____   _____   _____
_____   _____   _____
_____   _____   _____

🧁 Snack

_____

━━━━━ Water Intake ━━━━━
[ ] [ ] [ ] [ ] [ ] [ ] [ ] [ ] [ ]

_____

━━━━━ Hunger Scale ━━━━━
1   2   3   4   5   6   7   8   9   10
starving   So Full

_____

━━━━━ I Ate Because ━━━━━
[ ] STARVING   [ ] CRAVINGS   [ ] TROUBLED   [ ] MOODY   [ ] NEED FUEL

┌─ Symptoms/Feelings Post Meal ──→ How Long After Meal? ─┐
[ ] STRONG   [ ] BLOATING   [ ] DIGESTIVE   [ ] < 1HOUR   [ ] 1 - 2 HOURS
[ ] FOCUSED   [ ] FOGGY MIND   [ ] OTHER _____

what? where? When? Why?

Is my worst-case scenario really likely to happen? _____
_____
_____
_____
_____
_____

Date: _____ Sleep Time: _____ 😄 🙂 😐 🙁 😣

☕ Breakfast   🌮 Lunch   🍲 Dinner

_____   _____   _____
_____   _____   _____
_____   _____   _____
_____   _____   _____

🧁 Snack

_____

_____ Water Intake _____

[9 water glasses]

_____

_____ Hunger Scale _____

1 2 3 4 5 6 7 8 9 10

_____

starving   So Full

_____ I Ate Because _____

☐ STARVING ☐ CRAVINGS ☐ TROUBLED ☐ MOODY ☐ NEED FUEL

Symptoms/Feelings Post Meal ➔ How Long After Meal?

☐ STRONG ☐ BLOATING ☐ DIGESTIVE ☐ < 1HOUR ☐ 1 - 2 HOURS

☐ FOCUSED ☐ FOGGY MIND ☐ OTHER _____

what? where? When? Why?

When was the last time I had a good laugh? _____

_____
_____
_____
_____
_____

Date: _____ Sleep Time: _____ 😁 🙂 😐 ☹️ 😣

☕ Breakfast   🌮 Lunch   🍝 Dinner

_____ _____ _____
_____ _____ _____
_____ _____ _____
_____ _____ _____
_____ _____ _____

🧁 Snack

_____

_____

_____

_____

—— Water Intake ——

🥛 🥛 🥛 🥛 🥛 🥛 🥛 🥛 🥛

—— Hunger Scale ——

1   2   3   4   5   6   7   8   9   10

starving   So Full

—— I Ate Because ——

☐ STARVING   ☐ CRAVINGS   ☐ TROUBLED   ☐ MOODY   ☐ NEED FUEL

— Symptoms/Feelings Post Meal ——→ How Long After Meal? —

☐ STRONG   ☐ BLOATING   ☐ DIGESTIVE   ☐ < 1HOUR   ☐ 1 - 2 HOURS

☐ FOCUSED   ☐ FOGGY MIND   ☐ OTHER _____

what? where? When? Why?

What would I be risking if I did some of the things that are outside
of my comfort zone? _____

_____

_____

_____

_____

Date: _____   Sleep Time: _____   😁 🙂 😐 🙁 😫

☕ Breakfast

_____
_____
_____
_____
_____

🌮 Lunch

_____
_____
_____
_____
_____

🍤 Dinner

_____
_____
_____
_____
_____

🧁 Snack

_____
_____
_____
_____

Water Intake

🥛 🥛 🥛 🥛 🥛 🥛 🥛 🥛 🥛

Hunger Scale

1   2   3   4   5   6   7   8   9   10

starving   So Full

I Ate Because

☐ STARVING   ☐ CRAVINGS   ☐ TROUBLED   ☐ MOODY   ☐ NEED FUEL

Symptoms/Feelings Post Meal ➔ How Long After Meal?

☐ STRONG   ☐ BLOATING   ☐ DIGESTIVE   ☐ < 1HOUR   ☐ 1 - 2 HOURS

☐ FOCUSED   ☐ FOGGY MIND   ☐ OTHER _____

what? where? When? Why?

What is the single, most significant change I can make in this year? ——

_____
_____
_____
_____
_____

Date: _____ Sleep Time: _____ 😁 🙂 😐 ☹️ 😣

☕ Breakfast   🌮 Lunch   🍜 Dinner

_____   _____   _____
_____   _____   _____
_____   _____   _____
_____   _____   _____
_____   _____   _____

🧁 Snack

_____

_____

_____

_____

Water Intake

🥛 🥛 🥛 🥛 🥛 🥛 🥛 🥛 🥛

Hunger Scale

1   2   3   4   5   6   7   8   9   10

starving   So Full

I Ate Because

☐ STARVING   ☐ CRAVINGS   ☐ TROUBLED   ☐ MOODY   ☐ NEED FUEL

Symptoms/Feelings Post Meal ➡️ How Long After Meal?

☐ STRONG   ☐ BLOATING   ☐ DIGESTIVE   ☐ < 1HOUR   ☐ 1 - 2 HOURS

☐ FOCUSED   ☐ FOGGY MIND   ☐ OTHER _____

what? where? When? Why?

I wish I could _____
_____
_____
_____
_____

Date: _____ Sleep Time: _____ 😄 🙂 😐 🙁 😣

☕ Breakfast   🌮 Lunch   🍳 Dinner

_____   _____   _____
_____   _____   _____
_____   _____   _____
_____   _____   _____
_____   _____   _____

🧁 Snack

_____

_____

_____

—— Water Intake ——

🥛 🥛 🥛 🥛 🥛 🥛 🥛 🥛 🥛

—— Hunger Scale ——

1 2 3 4 5 6 7 8 9 10

starving   So Full

—— I Ate Because ——

☐ STARVING   ☐ CRAVINGS   ☐ TROUBLED   ☐ MOODY   ☐ NEED FUEL

— Symptoms/Feelings Post Meal ——➤ How Long After Meal? —

☐ STRONG   ☐ BLOATING   ☐ DIGESTIVE   ☐ < 1HOUR   ☐ 1 - 2 HOURS

☐ FOCUSED   ☐ FOGGY MIND   ☐ OTHER _____

what? where? When? Why?

One of the most important things I learned was _____

_____

_____

_____

_____

I may be the only person left who believes in me, but it's enough. It takes just one star to pierce a universe of darkness, Failure will never overtake me if my determination to succeed is strong enough.
(Og Mandino -Richelle E)

	Yes	No
Did I achieve My goals	☐	☐
I will use this journal again	☐	☐
Is it worth a good review	☐	☐

Made in the USA
Columbia, SC
16 December 2023

28749615R00063